"Stivers and van der Laan show
are and how deeply religious ou
confuse the United States' religic
tice. Despite this unholy alliance of religion and politics in pursuit
of power that leads to violence, our life in a technological system
is not hopeless. . . . This important book helps make sense both
of our current moment and the future we are collectively walking
towards."

—PAUL STOCK, Associate Professor of Sociology and the
Environmental Studies Program, University of Kansas

"In this lucid study, Stivers and van der Laan argue persuasively
that religion in America is in a precarious state, not so much for
lack of numbers or zeal, but for substituting religion for politics,
technology (and its product, consumption), or secular, personalist
approaches to spirituality. Above all, religion has distanced itself
from Scripture."

—JOHN PAUL RUSSO, Chair, Department of Classics,
University of Miami

"As the modern world surrenders itself to technological domination, modern religion predictably follows suit. Stivers and van der
Laan astutely dissect the blatant idolatry embedded within today's
technological religious options. Whether you choose technology's
offerings of political or personal religion, or a combination of both,
the biblical gospel of Jesus Christ remains irreconcilable to personal preference. *Religion in America Today* offers a much-needed
prophetic warning against the religious darkness that accompanies
technological 'illumination.'"

—DAVID M. CRUMP, New Testament professor, retired,
Calvin University

"Stivers and van der Laan have delivered a lean but muscular critical masterpiece. . . . Their analysis of today's impassioned, partisan
politics and its colonization of the Christian churches—and their
deep understanding of our technological milieu and its uncritical

embrace by pastors and churches—should be required reading by all pastors and seminary students. . . . Stivers and van der Laan speak truth to our reality, and the issues they raise must get on the agenda of any leader who cares about the church and the world."

—DAVID W. GILL, President, International Jacques Ellul Society

Religion in America Today

# Religion in America Today

*Richard Stivers*
*and J. M. van der Laan*

CASCADE *Books* · Eugene, Oregon

RELIGION IN AMERICA TODAY

Cascade Books
An Imprint of Wipf and Stock Publishers
199 W. 8th Ave., Suite 3
Eugene, OR 97401

www.wipfandstock.com

PAPERBACK ISBN: 978-1-7252-9313-7
HARDCOVER ISBN: 978-1-7252-9308-3
EBOOK ISBN: 978-1-7252-9312-0

*Cataloguing-in-Publication data:*

Names: Stivers, Richard, author. Van der Laan, J. M., author.

Title: Religion in America today / Richard Stivers and J. M. van der Laan.

Description: Eugene, OR: Cascade Books, 2021 | Includes bibliographical references.

Identifiers: ISBN 978-1-7252-9313-7 (paperback) | ISBN 978-1-7252-9308-3 (hardcover) | ISBN 978-1-7252-9312-0 (ebook)

Subjects: LCSH: Church and the world. | Ellul, Jacques, 1912–1994. | Christianity and social problems. | Culture conflict—United States.

Classification: BR115.W6 .R46 2021 (print) | BR115.W6 (ebook)

Dedication

To my wife of fifty-five years, Janet, a woman of great
compassion for those in need.

And

For my wife, Nancy.

# Contents

# Acknowledgments

JAMES VAN DER LAAN and Richard Stivers are heavily indebted to the secular and Christian work of Jacques Ellul, whose ideas and life have been an inspiration to us. Without his writings, which always forced us to apply them to our own times and lives, we could not have written this book. The authors wish to thank Sharon Foiles, who prepared the manuscript for the publisher. She has been a delight to work with for many years.

# Introduction

## The Enigma of Religion

THE CULTURAL SCIENCES INFORM us about the *reality* of religion, Scripture about the *truth* of religion. Without Scripture we are left with only an empirical view of religion; without the cultural sciences, a truth that is unspecified for our time. Just as truth is higher than reality so too is Scripture higher than the cultural sciences. Yet both are needed to understand religion.

Few subjects are as controversial as religion. Is religion a human creation, or did God create religion? Is there a true religion? Is religion primarily a form of social control and thus antithetical to freedom? Does religion promote love at the same time it results in violence? Is religion reducible to morality, and should that morality be imposed on nonbelievers? These are but a few of the questions that arise in any discussion of religion.

## What the Cultural Sciences Teach Us about Religion

Does religion meet an inherent individual need or a societal need? Some have argued that human nature includes a need for absolute meaning that only religion can provide, and some have even reduced this need to the biological level.[1] Others have emphasized

1. Lewontin, *Biology as Ideology*. Biological determinism is unscientific;

the part religion plays in the collective life of society. The history of the social sciences has witnessed a debate between individualism—society is only a loose collection of individuals—and collectivism—society totally determines the lives of individuals, reducing them to ciphers. Most social scientists, however, maintain a position that social determinants vary in intensity according to historical and social context. Individuals emerge in the struggle to resist these determinations if only to shape them to their own purposes.

René Girard argues that desire itself is mimetic, that is, we desire things because we wish to imitate, be like, others who desire them. He terms this "mimetic desire" and has made it the foundation of his theory of ritual scapegoating.[2] Fear and desire are simultaneously individual and social. The need for absolute meaning that the individual appears to need and society attempts to provide is social as well as individual. The meaning of existence that religion defines has to be lived in concert with others or it is hollow.

Religion, it is often argued, is the fundamental institution of society. It provides society with shared meaning and is a form of social control. The former entails a set of beliefs, the latter, normative direction in everyday life. Social institutions or cultural systems are culture applied to the various functions of society, such as marriage and procreation, law and justice, householding and trade, and ultimate beliefs. The normative dimension may be either moral or ritualistic. An institution relates to both material and spiritual needs and actions. It is at once practical and symbolic.

An institution specifies status and a division of labor in a hierarchy of authority. An institution delimits the extent of power exercised in authority and legitimates it. Those under the control of an institution do not typically question the authority itself but

moreover, it is an ideological reflection of a technological society in reducing all reality to what can be readily measured and controlled. If moral and political problems are ultimately only biological problems, then a technological solution is in the offing.

2. Girard, *Scapegoat.*

only its abuse. Institutions are not static. Tradition changes as circumstances change. Often the changes are so subtle that they are almost imperceptive, with the result that the traditions an institution gives rise to seem permanent.[3] The Constitution of the United States appears, with the exception of amendments, to be the same from the eighteenth century until today. But upon closer inspection we discover that as the Constitution is applied to new circumstances it changes, or should we say, is changed.

The institution of religion has historically assumed many forms, including mystery religions, ecstatic religions, ascetic religions, mystical religions, and moral philosophies. Categories of religion are not mutually exclusive, and some religions change categories historically so that for instance, a mystical emphasis gives way to an ascetic concentration.

As societies grow in size and technology develops, they become more highly differentiated. The division of labor between women and men and between old and young is superseded by an increasingly complex system of statuses and roles. Religious hierarchy is in keeping with the complexity of statuses in other institutions. A hierarchy of professional clergy becomes the norm.[4]

Whereas leadership is spontaneous and informal in new religious sects, if they are to survive to the next generation, the sects have to organize for the future—become institutionalized. Leadership based on virtue is supplanted by formal education and training. When bureaucracy becomes the dominant form of organization, religion embraces it. Auguste Comte, the "father of sociology," an avowed atheist, admired the bureaucratic organization of the Catholic Church in the nineteenth century, anticipating that social scientists would replace clergy in the new "scientific" bureaucracy.

In prehistory a division of labor between religion and politics was nonexistent. The tribe was a single religious and political entity, held together by myth and ritual. The tribe, it was believed, descended from the ancestors, who, present at the creation of

3. Sahlins, *Islands of History.*
4. Wach, *Sociology of Religion.*

the world, were demigods. There was no religious or political pluralism.

With the advent of founded religions, those with a historically recorded founder, e.g., the Prophet Mohammed of Islam, new religions burst into previously homogeneous societies, creating religious and political conflict. Eventually a single religion becomes the exclusive or at least favored state religion.

The nexus between religion and politics is tight. The division of labor between religion and politics grew with the increasing complexity of society to the point that political and religious governance each became full time. Political leaders, however, still had a role to play in religious activities and religious leaders in politics.

The example of medieval Christianity is apt. When Christianity became dominant in the West in the eleventh century, its religious and political-military leaders came from the same aristocratic families. The bishop and titled aristocrat held the same goal—to unite Christendom and empire. Knights and vassals were confirmed in religious ceremonies, and the aristocracy held a prominent place in church. Clearly the Church faced an enormous obstacle in bringing the political-military aristocracy, which practiced the heroic virtues of courage, loyalty, and pride under the control of a Christian morality, which emphasized the virtues of love and humility.

An attempt to prevent political and religious leaders from engaging in endless disputes was the ideal of the "Three Orders."[5] It was never fully realized in practice, however. An order pertained to a function, and the three orders constituted a hierarchy of functions (all of which were important). The highest function was prayer, which the clergy performed. The second order was military and political defense, which the aristocracy carried out. The third order was the function of labor, and its participants were all those not included in the first two orders. Aristocrats did not take kindly to being subordinate to bishops and the pope. The king's role in the Three Orders ingeniously included both the religious and the political-military functions—he alone was a prayer and a fighter.

5. Duby, *The Three Orders.*

But because the function of prayer was higher than that of military activity, the king was expected to consult the local bishop about the exercise of political-military power, especially about military conflict between two Christian societies.

The ideal of the Three Orders never took hold. There were exceptions: King Louis of France was considered a saint in his lifetime,[6] and the pope was able on occasion to force a wayward aristocrat to make a pilgrimage to Rome as reparation for his unchristian political or military action. But intrigue, dissension, and competition were the rule. Sometimes aristocrats were able to control the appointment of a bishop, and sometimes the pope exercised considerable influence in political matters without regard to his religious function. The convergence of religion and the state was exemplified in the king being regarded as a sacred person, apart from his religious functions. As the most powerful person in society, the king was a demigod.

The separation of church and state is rare in practice (even if an ideology promotes it) and is transitory. The main reason is that both institutions are a source of authority. The authority of religion is spiritual and moral, that of the state, legal. There is no way in practice, however, to separate the spiritual and the material, the ideal and the real. Each is dependent on the other for the legitimate exercise of power.

Religion appears to be a universal institution in society, but not without qualification. In prehistory tribes did not possess formally organized religions, that is, rationally constructed religions. Tribal members were religious, but their spontaneous beliefs were expressed in myth and ritual. Metaphor not logic was the means of understanding their place in the world. The tribe had the experience of the sacred without producing a systematic religion. Religion is one form a sense of the sacred can assume. We will see in chapter 3 that the sacred is experienced as that which is most powerful, most real, and thus of greatest value. The sacred is the foundation of all religions, informal and formal.

---

6. Duby, *Age of the Cathedrals.*

In the twentieth century social scientists began to investigate what came to be called "secular religion." Secular religions (see chapter 3) are ersatz religions that don't go by the name of religion but meet the same needs and serve the same functions that traditional religions do. These include personal and political religions. If we number informal religion in prehistory and secular religion in post-history (the technological environment wherein technology supplants experience, wisdom, and a living past), then religion appears to be universal. If religion is universal, is there a way to define it?

In perhaps the most widely cited definition of religion, anthropologist Clifford Geertz attempted to capture the essential dimensions of any religion:

> Religion is a system of symbols which acts to establish powerful, pervasive, and long-lasting moods and motivations in men by formulating conceptions of a general order of existence and clothing those conceptions with such an aura of factuality that the moods and motivations seem uniquely realistic.[7]

Geertz's definition emphasizes not only the symbolism of religion but its rational purpose and emotional impact and its claim to bring reality to an ideal state. Ritual, it is believed, makes the real and ideal one, if only temporarily. The desired outcome can be either positive, e.g., a bountiful crop, or negative, e.g., the avoidance of a famine. For Geertz ritual is the fundamental part of religion in its attempt to transform reality into an ideal state. Performed in the company of family, friends, and community, who indicate its approval, ritual motivates the initiate into the inner circle of believers. Ritual is perceived to be efficacious, but its true success is its ability to integrate individuals into the community. The emotional impact of ritual is the foundation of its normative control of members of society.

So, does Geertz's definition fit all religions, including informal and secular religions? It does only at a highly abstract level. The

7. Geertz, "Religion as a Cultural System," 70.

more abstract a definition or concept in the cultural sciences, the less meaning it provides. And meaning is dependent on context.

Judaism and Christianity are based on faith, not ritual. The latter works automatically and is objective. In creating cohesion in a community, it is collective. Belief is conformity to the group. Ritual creates order in society. By contrast, faith is subjective, that is, a gift from a personal God; it is not a possession, but a self-conscious relationship that leaves God and the believer free. Faith does not allow one to control God, our environment, or others. Although faith is to be lived out in a community of believers, it is radically individual. It removes one from the crowd before permitting one to form a community of the faithful. It beckons each individual to a life of free obedience. Faith is freedom, ritual is conformity. Faith is the acknowledgment that a personal God accompanies humans in life and human history.

Faith makes Judaism and Christianity unique. This is not intended as an apologetic statement, for unique does not mean true. The truth of faith is encapsulated in faith. The latter cannot be directly communicated to another. It has to be lived out and transmitted to another by the work of the Holy Spirit. Throughout its history, however, Christianity has most often acted as a religion based on ritual, that is, become an institution in society whose main purpose was moral control.[8] This has led some to call for a "religion-less" Christianity or what Barth called "true religion."[9]

## What Scripture Teaches Us about Religion

The institution of religion helps to allay fear and offers the promise of realized desires. Moreover, it provides collective meaning and is a source of social control. Religion appears to be necessary for our well-being. What does Scripture say about religion?

---

8. Ellul, *The Subversion of Christianity*.

9. Barth, *Church Dogmatics*, Vol. I, Part 2.

God's creation includes certain institutions such as marriage, law, and the state.[10] These institutions do not and cannot fully embody what is good according to God. They are necessary to maintain some degree of order so that human existence is tolerable. In numerous places in Scripture, Paul, Peter, and others urge Christians to obey the law and political authority. Nowhere do they claim these institutions are good in themselves; rather they are necessary and we should obey them unless they assert their absolute spiritual value and thus undermine God's will. Paul goes so far as to "uphold" the institution of slavery. Clearly it is not good in the sense of God's will. But he admonishes Christian masters and slaves to act in love in relation to one another, thereby suggesting that the abolition of slavery should not be their priority. His idea is that the practice of Christian love will undermine the power relationship in slavery. Institutions must be opposed, however, when they are regarded as spiritual powers, that is, idols. In some Christian circles today, for instance, the family has become sacred, an idol.

Is religion one of the institutions God created? No! Scripture regards religion, morality, and magic as idolatrous and thus sinful.[11] Morality and magic are invariably related to religion, to what humans regard as sacred. The sacred (chapter 3) is a human creation that has nothing to do with God being holy.[12] The sacred is mainly about power (not love), which has both positive and negative dimensions. The sacred refers to both good and evil, for instance. In the theory of the sacred, good (creation) springs from evil (chaos). This runs counter to the creation accounts in Genesis. Chaos, Satan, and the devil are not evil gods and the source of creation; instead they refer to sin. In Judaism and Christianity there is only one God, he who loves and liberates humans from sin. In rejecting God humans pursue their own evil course of action.

The sacred is the source of idolatry. Based as it is on the sacred, religion is idolatrous. Scripture indicates that God not only

10. Ellul, *Theological Foundation of Law.*

11. Ellul, *Freedom, Love, and Power.*

12. Snaith, *Distinctive Ideas of the Old Testament.*

creates humans but sustains them in a spiritual relationship that even sin does not fully destroy. Sin destroys the reciprocal relationship with God, leaving behind what Søren Kierkegaard termed "anxiety." Anxiety is a state of disquiet in which the sinner cannot rid himself of the relationship, nor readily make it whole once again.[13] Anxiety is unrecognized sin: Only scripture can reveal sin for what it is—a broken relationship with God. Yet God maintains a relationship with the sinner, and that is what causes the (dis)ease of the spirit.

The following example is an imaginary use of Kierkegaard. Anxiety, the disease of the spirit, can be compared (in a limited way) to a romantic relationship in which one person breaks up with the other. The one who was the "victim" of the breakup keeps loving the one who abandoned the relationship, however. When the two run across each other, or perhaps only the name of the former lover is mentioned, the one who broke off the relationship experiences unconscious anxiety, even guilt, about the abandoned relationship, the more so the abandoned one maintains a loving relationship with her. Love does not require both parties love each other, only one. God's love continues unabated despite our attempt to end the relationship.

In their anxious, sinful condition, humans create religion. It becomes a means of justifying oneself to God, a means of asserting one's self-righteousness in piety, and of reconciling God to the world.[14] Idolatry is either the cause or the result of sinful self-justification, most likely both.[15] Most often Christian idolatry makes the church sacred. In capturing God's word and objectifying it, the church in the form of a religious organization makes itself equal to God. The need for religion is a consequence of sin. As the external manifestation of spiritual disease, religion varies historically and culturally.

---

13. Kierkegaard, *Concept of Anxiety*; see also Kierkegaard, *Sickness Unto Death*.

14. Barth, *Church Dogmatics*, Vol. I, Part 2.

15. Barth, *Church Dogmatics*, Vol. I, Part 2, 310.

If religion is not an institution created by God, perhaps morality is. But morality is invariably derived from the institution of religion, from a belief in the sacred. In Genesis there are two trees: the tree of life and the tree to discern good from evil. Scripture reveals that the good is God's will, which can never be objectified as moral law or moral philosophy.

Following Barth, a commandment is not an abstract, universal norm.[16] A commandment is the permission to live out one's faith in a specific context, addressed to specific individuals and groups. No generalization is possible; moreover, each commandment has to be understood in relation to all other commandments. Even though a commandment applies to each believer, prayer and grace are necessary to ascertain what the commandment means for me in my circumstances. The believer never owns God's will but remains dependent on the living word. Ellul argues that a Christian ethic, then, should be indicative rather than prescriptive and proscriptive.[17] Christ's words and actions are an indication of how we should behave, but indications that have to be applied to the context of our own lives. Objectifying the various commands God gives us creates a morality that reduces God's expectations to our own presuppositions and desire for a comfortable moral existence.

Throughout Scripture prophets and disciples who performed miracles were challenged by magicians. The two are radically different. A miracle is not primarily a spectacular, unexplained occurrence, but the work of God. The birth of faith, almost imperceptible, is the greatest miracle. Magic, by contrast, is the attempt to control a sacred power, to bend its will to ours.[18] Magic is recognized by its external outcome, miracle by the internal recognition of its source—God. Magic is most often performed in a ritualistic setting. Ritual is essentially magical in its attempt to transform reality into an ideal state. For Geertz, as we have seen, ritual is the heart of religion: Religion is necessarily ritualistic.

16. Barth, *Church Dogmatics*, Vol. II, Part 2.

17. Ellul, *To Will and to Do*.

18. Stivers, *Technology as Magic*.

If religion, morality, and magic were not created by God, why are they as prevalent as the institutions of law, government, and marriage that God created? Scripture indicates that God wants us to live in a secular society, a society whose institutions were of relative, not absolute, value. Religion, morality, and magic are sinful attempts to create substitutes for God—idols—and thereby avoid anxiety and sin and feel justified and self-righteous. Certainly law, government, and marriage can be infused with a sacred quality, but they are not sacred institutions when they retain the relative value they have as God's creation. Religion, morality, and magic inherently derive from idolatry and consequently can never be secular. Religion is both necessary and sinful. It is necessary because in their sinful condition humans refuse to repent so that the broken relationship with God can be made whole once again. Consequently, religion becomes the cornerstone of society. God in turn tolerates religion, morality, and magic as necessary evils in his great love for humanity.

How can Christianity avoid becoming a religion? Paul was continually bringing various churches back to Christ's true teachings. The question could just as well be put: How does the church avoid idolatry? The struggle is enormous, and left to itself the church will fail. Paul equates covetousness with idolatry.[19] Ellul argues that at its base sin is covetousness.[20] The upshot is that sin is less a moral offense than a spiritual one. When we sin, we turn something in the world into an idol. How does the church avoid religion is tantamount to asking how does it avoid sin. The church needs to be organized around the gifts of the Holy Spirit and leadership based on faith. The moment the informal organization of the church becomes formal, institutionalized, and bureaucratized, there is no room for the Holy Spirit. Objectification of Scripture is a way of laying hold of God for our ease. The freedom of God's word escapes human control.

The world is the home of the sacred, the church the home of faith in God. When religion invades the church, it is really the

19. Col 3:5
20. Ellul, *Son of God.*

world taking hold. In Part I of this book, "The Church of the World," James van der Laan examines how the sacred entities, technology and the political state have influenced church practices. In Part 2, "The World as Church," Richard Stivers analyzes the kinds of secular religions that these sacred entities have given rise to: personal religion and political religion. The Conclusion discusses how Christianity as a religion is forced to make its living within these secular religions. The resulting syncretism makes Christianity subservient to these secular religions or, in other words, a slave of the world and its idols. This book represents one attempt to "discern the spirits," in this instance, our modern idols.

# PART I

*The Church of the World*

CHAPTER 1

# The Church and the State

*Do not put your trust in princes, in mortal men, who cannot save.*
*When their spirit departs, they return to the ground; on that very*
*day their plans come to nothing.*

—PSALM 146:3-4

THE COALITION OF THE Christian church and the secular state has
a long history. Let a brief review suffice. The close relationship was
first forged by Emperor Theodosius who by edict in 380 AD made
Christianity, as defined by the council that Emperor Constantine
had convened fifty-five years earlier in Nicaea, the Roman Empire's
state religion. When Pope Leo III crowned Charlemagne in 800, he
became not only a new as it were Roman emperor, but also the
sovereign of Christendom. Throughout the Middle Ages, the state
sought the church's blessing for its rulers and their undertakings,
while the church sought to extend its power into the affairs of the
state. In 1555, because of problems caused by the Reformation, the
Peace of Augsburg in 1555 declared *cuius regio, ejus religio*, a deter-
mination that allowed the head of each state to dictate the religion
of his land. With the Enlightenment and the emergence of democratic, republican government, new states formed and excluded
the church from participation in the political realm. For example,

the French Revolution led to a short-lived separation of church and state, but Napoleon terminated that policy when he came to power. In 1791, the United States explicitly forbade "the establishment of religion" in the first amendment to its Constitution. The Bill of Rights, where that amendment appears, seemed to guarantee the separation of church and state. While the US has no official state religion, church and state nevertheless found ways to cooperate.

In 1835, Alexis de Tocqueville published the first volume of *On Democracy in America*. There he described an intimate relation of church and state which had already developed:

> The greatest part of British America was peopled by men who, after having shaken off the authority of the Pope acknowledged no other religious supremacy: they brought with them into the New World a form of Christianity which I cannot better describe than by styling it a democratic and republican religion. This contributed powerfully to the establishment of a republic and democracy in public affairs; and from the beginning, politics and religion contracted an alliance which has never been dissolved.[1]

Almost two hundred years have passed since he wrote those words, and the collaboration he detected then has persisted to the present day.

This essay does not reexamine the relationship between church and state over the course of American history. For such an overview, see Edward S. Gaustad's *Church and State in America* (2d edition 2003) or James H. Hutson's *Church and State in America: The First Two Centuries* (2008). In these pages, the focus falls rather on the first two decades of the twenty-first century, and specifically on the error of the Christian church in its close association with the state and in its profane pursuit of ends by political means. Americanized Christians desire and even celebrate the collaboration of church and state, as do certain politicians who have recognized its benefits for themselves and their party. From a

---

1. Tocqueville, *On Democracy*, vol. I, 311.

Christian standpoint, however, such a union is insupportable and unacceptable. The problem is not so much that Americans have a civic religion, as that the Christian church has sought and accepted a role in it.

Arguments about the separation of church and state erupt periodically in the US, especially when secular voices object to the presence of religious symbols or texts on state-owned property. Crosses, Christmas displays, or the Ten Commandments at city halls or county courthouses draw the ire of the secular community, but many Christians insist on such religious exhibits. Conversely, it is not at all unusual to find Christian churches, representing various denominations in the United States, with the national flag standing prominently in their sanctuaries. On national holidays, such as Memorial Day, the Fourth of July, or Veterans Day, churches often hold special patriotic services and sing songs like "America the Beautiful," "The Battle Hymn of the Republic," "My Country tis of Thee," "God Bless America," "God Bless the USA," and even "The Star Spangled Banner," to name but a few of them. As Kate Shellnut reported in 2018 in *Christianity Today*, "a majority of Protestant pastors (61 percent) believe it's important to celebrate the country around July 4," and do so even though "they also recognize the tensions at hand." Many pastors felt that "their congregation sometimes seems to love America more than God."[2] While few Americanized Christians think twice about pledging allegiance to the flag and the nation-state for which it stands, early Christians were martyred for refusing to pledge allegiance to anyone or anything else but their triune God. *Americanized* Christians somehow think they can serve two masters.

In the United States, both religious and political leaders have conflated and confused Christianity with nationalism and patriotism for the country which in turn equates with an endorsement of free-market economics, consumer capitalism, a strong military, and American exceptionalism. Some may recall how, as president, George W. Bush appropriated the words of the gospel in a speech on the first anniversary of the September 11, 2001 terrorist attacks

2. Shellnut, "Make Worship Patriotic Again?"

against the United States. He used John 1:5—"The light shines in the darkness, but the darkness has not overcome it"—to describe *not* the presence of God, but of the United States in the world. *Not* Jesus Christ, but the USA becomes the hope and savior of the world.

Something we might call a *Christian Americanism* or *Americanized Christianity* has now asserted itself, by which I mean a religious orientation strongly influenced by a thoroughly American social, economic, and political agenda that affects both domestic and foreign policy. Andrew Whitehead and Samuel Perry call it *Christian nationalism.* In their book *Taking America Back for God,* they document the belief that "American civic life" should be blended or fused "with a particular type of Christian identity and culture."[3] As they explain, Christian nationalism is political at its core, and it "has thoroughly permeated American society and culture."[4] A majority of American Christians, they determined, overtly seek and cultivate a union of church and state. In this union, Christian religion yields to conservative politics, love for country vies with and comes before love for God and the neighbor. For them, religious freedom means the freedom to establish a certain kind of Christianity as the religion of America, despite the first amendment to the US Constitution.

The admixture of God and country, where country actually comes before God, must be challenged. Many Americanized Christians want and welcome the opportunity to participate in the political, as they have felt themselves too long excluded from such activity. Prominent voices in the church on the one hand, elected state and federal officials on the other, have continued to promote such an unholy alliance. A large block of Americanized Christians has seen fit to make common cause in particular with a Republican party shaped over the years largely by the likes of Ronald Reagan, Newt Gingrich, Karl Rove, Dick Cheney, and more recently Mitch McConnell, William Barr, Mike Pompeo, and Donald Trump—a party with a decidedly secular politics that owes little or nothing

3. Whitehead and Perry, *Taking America Back*, ix–x.
4. Whitehead and Perry, *Taking America Back*, 18.

to the teachings of Jesus. While so-called liberal Christians have tended to support the Democratic party, a party with an equally secular political agenda, they have not pressed for or endorsed such extensive church and state cooperation as have conservative Christians who back Republican politicians. For this reason, most of the examples to follow come from American evangelicals and the more conservative-minded Christians in the United States.

There are many who consider the United States a Christian nation, and a great many Americans consider themselves Christians. About 65 percent of the population in the United States in 2019 (down from about 75 percent in 2015), in other words, the vast majority of Americans, defined themselves as Christian. According to the Pew Research Center, evangelical Protestants (25.4 percent) and Roman Catholics (20.8 percent) make up the largest portion of Christians in the US, while mainline Protestants account for only 14.7 percent, and historically black Protestants another 6.5 percent.[5] In 2008, at least 84.8 percent of the 111th United States Congress identified as Christian (55.7 percent Protestant, 30.1 percent Roman Catholic), and 91 percent and 88 percent of the last two congresses, the 115th and 116th respectively, identified as Christian.[6] Those numbers do not, however, make the nation Christian, and the teachings of Jesus have not determined public policy. Neither goodness and mercy nor love and compassion for fellow human beings receive much, if any consideration, when the stakes are political. For committed Christians, any merger of church and state must be at odds with their professed beliefs, as a comparison of Christian scriptural teachings with any policies of the American nation-state (regardless of the political party in power) must immediately reveal. Centuries ago, Tertullian asked rhetorically, "what has Jerusalem to do with Athens?" contrasting the thought and action of the church with that of the world. The answer must be a clear and simple: nothing.

Over the years, the so-called evangelicals in this country have tended especially to engage with the state, and the National

---

5. Pew Forum, "Religious Landscape Study."
6. Pew Forum, "Faith on the Hill."

Association of Evangelicals has become ever more instrumental in extending the political power of its members. In *Jesus and John Wayne: How White Evangelicals Corrupted a Faith and Fractured a Nation*, Kristin Kobes Du Mez traced how the movie star became the model of manliness for evangelicals, someone who reveres the military and patriarchal power. Although she is primarily concerned with the emergence of an aggressive, tough, warrior-like masculinity, she found as well that American evangelicals identify with a theology that is "Republican in its politics," "traditionalist in its values," and have a God-and-country faith.[7] These evangelicals advance "their agenda through strategic organizations and political alliances, on occasion by way of ruthless displays of power."[8] But she also documented how the National Association of Evangelicals became a political power, proclaiming a message of Christian Americanism. "Weaving together intimate family matters, domestic politics, and a foreign policy agenda, militant masculinity came to reside at the heart of a larger evangelical identity," she determined.[9] She notes that "despite evangelicals' frequent claims that the Bible is the source of their social and political commitments, evangelicalism must be seen as a cultural and political movement rather than as a community defined by its theology."[10]

In the first decade of this century, Pastor Ted Haggard was the minister of the huge Colorado Springs New Life Church and president of the National Association of Evangelicals. In 2005, *Time Magazine* labeled him one of the most influential religious leaders in America.[11] At the same time, Haggard publicly aligned himself with the politics of Republican George W. Bush. He stood in all but full agreement with that president, except for which brand of pickup truck to drive—one was a Chevy, the other a Ford man. Indeed, so closely connected was Haggard to the Bush

7. Du Mez, *Jesus and John Wayne*, 7.
8. Du Mez, *Jesus and John Wayne*, 9.
9. Du Mez, *Jesus and John Wayne*, 295.
10. Du Mez, *Jesus and John Wayne*, 298.
11. *Time*, "The 25 Most Influential Evangelicals."

administration that it had his cell phone number—and called it.[12] Haggard's relationship with the politics of George W. Bush reflects how intimate the coalition of church and state had become. And as Du Mez observes, Haggard's Christianity was "explicitly political."[13] She goes on to note that he supported the preemptive war in Iraq, and "embraced free-market capitalism both as an economic model and as essential to the spread of Christianity."[14]

Haggard's own presidential message on the NAE website in 2006 deserves some attention here, as it suggests the political clout he wanted the church to exercise. Here are his opening words: "The NAE is composed of fifty-three member denominations representing 45,000 churches across America; our numbers generate influence and power . . . . Together we can accomplish more than we could ever achieve on our own. And now is the time to prove it."[15] The paragraph is remarkable for at least two reasons: for its emphasis on numbers, influence, and power on the one hand, and for its aggressive, almost threatening tone on the other. The notion of the church as a remnant and an understanding of Christ as the embodiment of non-power has here been swept aside. But to seek power of any kind is, as Jacques Ellul pointed out in his book *Apocalypse*, always to "turn away from God."[16]

Haggard's second paragraph takes up freedom, not freedom as defined in and by Christ, but by Ronald Reagan, the venerated hero of the Republican party. According to Haggard quoting Reagan, freedom "is never more than one generation away from extinction." This statement blurs the distinction between church and state, as it implies that the church (or is it the state?) must defend some notion of freedom. Whatever this vague freedom is (personal, political, economic, religious?), it is definitely not Christian, not, as Ellul observed, "the liberty attested by the paschal Lamb as the meaning of history [which] is not the product of

12. See Sharlet, "Soldiers of Christ."

13. Du Mez, *Jesus and John Wayne*, 208.

14. Du Mez, *Jesus and John Wayne*, 208.

15. Haggard, "Presidential Message."

16. Ellul, *Apocalypse*, 138.

the accumulation of human powers but the intervention (*intervenire*), the mysterious insertion, of the Nonpower of God."[17] It is "a liberty given by God," not, as Reagan and Haggard implied, "made by man."[18]

In his third paragraph, Haggard's concern is still not Christ or the church per se, but the nation's armed forces. "Right now," Haggard continued, "the United States Air Force is being sued by a radical extremist who seeks to impose his views of secular humanism upon our men and women in uniform."[19] To speak of radical extremism suggests grave danger and incites fear. By bringing up the Air Force, Haggard inserts a nationalistic, political element into the concerns of the church. After all, the military is an extension of the nation-state dedicated to warfare and, as the German military theorist Carl von Clausewitz indicated, "war is not merely an act of policy, but a true political instrument, a continuation of political intercourse, carried on with other means. . . . The political object is the goal, war is the means of reaching it."[20] Haggard's declaration about the military hides a commitment to the political. He purposely blended and confused the kingdom of the world (America) with the kingdom of God. Since he published these remarks, Haggard has had to resign from the positions of power he held in 2006 as the result of a scandal, what the board of his New Life Church called sexually immoral conduct. However, he went on to found a new church, St. James, in Colorado Springs, where in 2010 he began to serve as pastor.

Also in 2010, the influential professor of theology and Biblical studies at Phoenix Seminary (Scottsdale, Arizona), Wayne Grudem, published *Politics According to the Bible: A Comprehensive Resource for Understanding Modern Political Issues in Light of Scripture*. With this book, Grudem offered Christians a guide with a specific political agenda for them to embrace and enact. However, contrary to his title's assertion, his political counsel aligns

---

17. Ellul, *Apocalypse*, 138.

18. Cf. Ellul, *Apocalypse*, 120.

19. Haggard, "Presidential Message."

20. Clausewitz, *On War*, 87.

more with the Republican party than with the Bible. For example, he maintains that the Bible gives support to democracy, private property, and free market capitalism as opposed to socialism or communism, that taxes should be lower for the rich and prosperous, that "originalist" judges should be appointed to the Supreme Court, and that the wars in Iraq and Afghanistan were justified. To shore up his "just cause" argument he repeated theories about weapons of mass destruction that have been fully discredited. While Grudem claims that the political convictions he recommends accord with Christian Scripture, he admits that he has not argued from "direct, specific Biblical teaching" on the topics in question.[21] In short, the Bible has little to do with his "biblical" politics. Instead, he has conflated a conservative American political program with Christianity. Grudem has been active in politics himself and has published recommendations or directives which, by virtue of his reputation as a theologian and seminary professor, some Christians could well deem authoritative. In 2016, Grudem argued in *Townhall* that Donald Trump was a morally good choice for president[22] and in 2020 endorsed him for president of the United States.

The mixture and confusion of church and state is both pervasive and banal. Attached to countless cars across the country (or at least throughout the Midwest), ubiquitous magnetic "ribbons" declared (or is it demanded?) "Support Our Troops" against a backdrop of the red, white, and blue of the nation's flag with the sign of the cross neatly blended in. Waiting in the watch repairman's shop several years ago, I heard Merle Haggard on the radio singing a country music song written by Gretchen Wilson called "Politically Uncorrect" (released in September 2005), giving voice to the perceived bond between God and country: "Nothing wrong with the Bible, / Nothing wrong with the flag." That verse presents a widespread attitude and a neat pairing of Christian religion and patriotism, while at the same time matter-of-factly asserting the idea that "American means Christian" and vice versa.

21. Grudem, *Politics According to the Bible*, 19.
22. Grudem, "Why Voting for Donald Trump."

As it happens, the sentiment expressed in that song has existed for some time. Gene Autry sang something similar in 1949 with "The Bible on the Table and the Flag upon the Wall." Now, T-shirts emblazoned with "I Stand for the Flag / I Kneel for the Cross" can be purchased. On Amazon, the product description and marketing blurb encourages potential buyers with: "Celebrate both your patriotism and your faith in God Almighty"; "Display your loyalty to America and reverence to God proudly."[23] With such attire, men and women make a statement about the homogeneity of God and country, but country comes first.

Politics, Jacques Ellul observed, "demands religion as an ally,"[24] but in this country religion demands politics as its ally as well. For many decades, the prominent evangelical Pat Robertson has enjoyed a substantial following and, thanks to his media empire, has exerted considerable influence. Disseminated by the powerful Christian Broadcasting Network, his *700 Club* continues to attract large audiences, and according to its website "can be seen in 96 percent of the homes in the U.S." with an estimated yearly worldwide viewing audience of 360 million people.[25] He professes to be a Christian and to speak as one, yet he has long had an overtly political agenda, one which serves a nationalistic and secular, rather than Christian or sacred purpose. He even sought for himself the Republican party's nomination for US president in 1988. After his personal bid for the presidency failed, Robertson founded the Christian Coalition a year later in order to promote a particular brand of politics. The organization was subsequently renamed the Christian Coalition of America in order to receive tax-exempt status. It claims to defend America's godly heritage, but "godly" hardly characterizes the history of the United States. As listed on its website, its main concerns in 2020 were, among others: the repeal and replacement of Obamacare, support for the nation of Israel, the reduction of government spending and debt, establishing peace through strong military policy, defense of

23. "Stand for the Flag."
24. Ellul, *Politics of God*, 126.
25. Christian Broadcasting Network, *The 700 Club*.

the Second Amendment right to bear arms, stopping the public funding of abortion, and opposition to so-called liberal judicial nominations.[26] The Coalition appears more interested in characteristically conservative political issues than the life and work of Jesus Christ.

Like Robertson, a media pundit and mogul, James Dobson is a prominent Christian voice in America. And like Haggard, he is based in Colorado Springs. He similarly reached huge audiences with his many media enterprises which emphasized family values and perhaps not so subtly celebrated and promoted America, not to mention the Republican party's policies and practices. According to Du Mez, Dobson's Focus on the Family "provided a critical fulcrum for evangelical political engagement."[27] As the Dobson organization focuses on the family, Jesus' own problematic statements about family call for comment. Family values may be desirable, but they are not inherently Christian. In addition to its Christian motivational and self-help materials, "Dr. James Dobson's Family Talk" has in the last few years presented broadcasts on such topics as: "Socialism: The Enemy of Christianity," by Jack Graham (March 30, 2020); "The Forgotten Promise of American Liberty," by Eric Metaxas (May 21, 2020); "Our Changing Role in Global Affairs," by Mike Pompeo (June 11, 2020); "America's Declaration of Independence," by Lloyd Ogilvie (July 20, 2020); "America: A Great Idea," by Tommy Nelson (January 25, 2019); "Unprecedented Times: Michele Bachmann on America's Foundation," by Michele Bachmann (March 18, 2019); "Valuing God and Country," by Tim Lee (May 1, 2020); and "Praying for Our Nation at War," by Oliver North (Memorial Day, May 27, 2019).[28] As this list demonstrates, the Dobson broadcast serves in effect as an instrument of propaganda for a Christian nationalism and

---

26. Christian Coalition of America. While that web page existed in September, it was no longer available in October of 2020. In any case, the agenda has changed little in the meantime. The new web address is https://cc.org/legislative-agenda/.

27. Du Mez, *Jesus and John Wayne*, 208.

28. Dobson, "Past Broadcasts."

patriotism, where Christianity and America blend together and become all but indistinguishable.

Currently, evangelical leaders like Franklin Graham and Jerry Falwell Jr., both sons of famous and influential evangelical preachers who had their own intimate ties with national politicians, have embraced political action and been outspoken, staunch supporters of Donald Trump. Falwell, for example, publicly endorsed Trump for the 2016 election, encouraging evangelical Christians to choose him on their ballots. (As of August 2020, Falwell's credibility might now be in question, since he became embroiled in a scandal that developed after he posted pictures of himself with a young woman, not his wife, each with their pants unzipped.) What is more, both Graham and Dobson have gone out of their way to defend and excuse Trump, his infidelities, abusive language, licentiousness, mendacity, dishonesty, irreverence, and arrogance, actions and behavior otherwise irreconcilable with Christian mores. As reported in *The Washington Post*, Trump "has said multiple times that he does not like to ask God for forgiveness."[29] When Arthur Brooks, quoting Jesus in Matthew 5:44, urged the audience at the 2020 national prayer breakfast to "love your enemies," Trump replied, "I don't know if I agree with you," an obfuscation used to conceal his rejection of Jesus' command. Such statements notwithstanding, Americanized Christians remained committed to the person and politics of Donald Trump.

Not only American evangelicals, but also Catholics have chosen the path of political action and influence. In 2005, CatholicVote.Org formed in order to promote a conservative politics, and by 2020, the coalition Catholics for Trump had emerged. According to a study by Jessica Martínez and Gregory A. Smith (also for the Pew Research Center) "fully eight-in-ten self-identified white, born-again/evangelical Christians say they voted for Trump" in the 2016 presidential election. Martínez and Smith documented very strong support for Trump among Catholics as well: 60 percent of white Catholics (52 percent of all Catholics) voted for him

---

29. Bailey, Zauzmer, and Dawsey, "Trump Mocks the Faith."

in 2016.[30] Both groups overwhelmingly chose and still support for president a man who lied relentlessly, whose yes did not mean yes, who had no compassion for the poor, dispossessed, and disenfranchised, and who sowed discord rather than peace, hate and enmity rather than love. In other words, the vast majority of Christians in America supported a man who embodied a political program which disdained the weak and suffering, fomented fear and hatred, and tolerated dishonesty and falsehood. And they did so enthusiastically. The Christian obligation to love the neighbor, to seek justice and mercy, to speak the truth, and to proclaim peace, forgiveness, and righteousness to the world falls by the wayside, when political motives and goals take precedent.

Granted, not all Christians seek political influence and power. And there are Christian voices in this country that question an Americanized Christianity, but they are in the minority. There was a group of Christians in 2004, for example, who signed a declaration written by Glen Stassen and Lewis Smedes, in which they raised objections to the policies and practices of the United States during the administration of George W. Bush. They were responding as well to the likes of Jerry Falwell Sr., who had proclaimed that "God is Pro-War" and Charles Stanley, pastor of the First Baptist Church of Atlanta and former president of the Southern Baptist Convention, who injudiciously announced that "we should offer to serve the war effort in any way possible."[31]

Based loosely on the 1934 Barmen Declaration (composed chiefly by Karl Barth in opposition to National Socialism), the 2004 statement, entitled "Confessing Christ in a World of Violence," had no great impact. In Christian circles, it received only minimal attention. Nevertheless, its resolutions speak against any kind of Christian nationalism: "Whenever Christianity compromises with empire, the gospel of Christ is discredited; We reject the false teaching that America is a 'Christian nation;' No nation-state may usurp the place of God; We reject the false teaching that any human being can be defined as outside the law's protection;

30. Martínez and Smith, "How the Faithful Voted."
31. Quoted by Marsh, "Wayward Christian Soldiers."

Peacemaking is central to our vocation in a troubled world where Christ is Lord."[32] In contrast and if their voting record was any indication, the vast majority of Americanized Christians found little, if anything wrong with the course of action chosen by the Bush administration.

In 2005, Jim Wallis published a book entitled *God's Politics: How the Right Gets It Wrong and the Left Doesn't Get It*. While grateful for and appreciative of the efforts by Wallis (and his magazine *Sojourners*), I wonder if he might not perhaps trust too much in what can be accomplished through the political process and so fall into the very trap Christians must avoid. Nevertheless, he correctly indicted both the conservative and liberal wings of the American electorate. In his book from 2006, *What Jesus Meant*, Garry Wills sharpened the focus and reminded Christians of what they all should already know: that Jesus subscribed to and offered no political program whatsoever. The hugely popular evangelical leader Beth Moore has spoken out via Twitter, on December 8, 2017, for example, to castigate Christians for selling their souls in order to buy political wins.[33] And in 2018, David Crump published *I Pledge Allegiance: A Believer's Guide to Kingdom Citizenship in Twenty-First-Century America,* in which he decried how Christians mistakenly placed their faith in the nation-state rather than in Jesus alone.

Crump shows that the church, when it approves and endorses the actions of the state, abandons its calling by and covenant with Christ. We may be citizens of the United States, but our true allegiance can only be to the kingdom of God as citizens of that kingdom. In the world (in the United States), we children of God can always and only be strangers and aliens.[34] As Crump reminds Christians, "the things that disciples of Jesus are called to do or not to do as citizens of God's kingdom are a far cry from the decision-making processes of secular government and public policy."[35]

32. Stassen and Smedes, "Confessing Christ."

33. Moore, Twitter.

34. Crump, *I Pledge Allegiance*, 67ff.

35. Crump, *I Pledge Allegiance*, 88.

Crump rejects Christian nationalism in the United States, because the kingdom of God "is never represented by any earthly nation, no matter what its character is."[36] As he notes, the only nation God ever made his covenant with was ancient Israel. The United States has not taken its place, nor can it do so,[37] because God's new covenant people are "the universal church of Jesus Christ, a community of faith spread throughout the world, . . . a countercultural people not of this world,"[38] hence not of the United States either. The church must reject "the numerous strategies that are offered for manipulating earthly power for kingdom purposes by grabbing the reins of government,"[39] if it is to remain faithful to the witness and gospel of its lord and savior.

In his book *The Politics of God and the Politics of Man*, Ellul examined the attempt to present the all-too-human political agenda as divine will and vice versa. Even though in his own life he thoroughly engaged with the world around him, Ellul argued against putting our hope in politics of any kind. While he wrote about persons and events recorded in the historical books of the Old Testament, Ellul's observations throw much needed light on the situation in the United States and especially on the alliance of the Christian church and the secular state. Of particular interest is what Ellul called "the sin of Jeroboam," the savvy and calculating king and politician who tried to use God to enhance the state.[40] That is, Jeroboam intentionally and deliberately blurred the distinction between the interests of God and those of the nation. Israel was certainly different from the other nations in the region, but Jeroboam chose his own political agenda over trust in the Lord. It is in that sense that we find a relation to Christians today who seek political solutions which have little to do with God's will.

In effect, Jeroboam wed and in doing so prostituted what can be considered the church at that time to the state. Leaders of the

36. Crump, *I Pledge Allegiance*, 118.
37. Crump, *I Pledge Allegiance*, 125.
38. Crump, *I Pledge Allegiance*, 126.
39. Crump, *I Pledge Allegiance*, 194.
40. Ellul, *Politics of God*, 88.

RELIGION IN AMERICA TODAY

Christian church, along with the political leaders of this country, have committed the same sin. (To be sure, this is not the first time in the history of the church that such collaboration has occurred.) As defined by Ellul, politics "consists in exact calculation and the power to intervene. . . . It is measured by the success of what it undertakes. It has its own goal."[41] Its goal is in no way identical with that of the church, however. "Values, sentiments, and opinions are among the given factors which the sagacious calculation of politics will take into consideration," he observed, "but there can be no question of achieving justice or truth by politics."[42] Even so, the church in America, whether liberal or conservative, looks to politics for such answers. For example, Christian conservatives want the state to legislate morality related to abortion and homosexuality, while Christian liberals want the state to legislate equality and respect for human rights. But as Ellul points out, "it is quite unbiblical to appeal to . . . political power. To do so is defiance of God *par excellence*. It is to reject God himself."[43] However, Christians in America desire political power and political solutions.

In *Living Faith*, Ellul assigned politics to the realm of the demonic. It has one purpose and goal, "the acquisition of power,"[44] an end incompatible with the non-power of Jesus Christ. Politics is diabolical and satanic in the way it *divides* (sows discord) and *accuses* opponents of all that is wrong in the world.[45] Religion itself becomes satanic "every time it has fallen into the grip of politics."[46] In the same way, the church in America has erred and allied itself with the devil (the divider) and the satan (the accuser), as it uses political means in its attempt to acquire power in order to achieve some purportedly "Christian" end. But politics pollute and corrupt the desired or imagined goal, so that nothing Christian remains to be achieved.

41. Ellul, *Politics of God*, 146.
42. Ellul, *Politics of God*, 146.
43. Ellul, *Politics of God*, 147–48.
44. Ellul, *Living Faith*, 235.
45. Ellul, *Living Faith*, 241.
46. Ellul, *Living Faith*, 241.

The separation of church and state does not entail inactivity on the part of Christians. "We need to live in and help evolve societies," Ellul wrote in *On Freedom, Love, and Power*; "we cannot do otherwise, but we must make sure a society never becomes an ideal or a sacred."[47] Americanized Christians have idealized and sacralized the United States, when they try to make it a *Christian* nation, when they believe it to be a nation chosen by God and set apart and above all others, and when they employ political means to achieve ends supposedly in the service of God. Christians may choose one political candidate or party over another, although Christians might well instead disengage from politics. In *The Political Illusion*, Ellul described the mistaken belief that someone "can modify reality itself in our day by the exercise of *political* power. The same illusion is held, though conversely, by those who think they can master and control the state by participating in the political game."[48] Christians must be *dis*-illusioned. They must disavow politics as a means to a Christian end, and they must reject the cooperation of church and state. As Ellul wrote in *The Subversion of Christianity*, Christians "must uphold the sure and certain fact that the Bible brings us a message that is against power, against the state, and against politics."[49]

Without doubt, Christians must be engaged in the world. In particular, Christians have a duty to confront the world and its values, to call the world to repentance and conversion, to proclaim God's love and forgiveness to the world, and in that way to have an effect on culture and society. After all, Christians are to be salt in the world, the yeast in the dough, that transforms the world, always to be *in*, but not *of*, the world. But Americanized Christians have chosen to be both in and of the world of politics. In *The Cost of Discipleship*, Dietrich Bonhoeffer addressed this very matter: let the Christian "remain in the world to engage in frontal assault on it, and let him live the life of his secular calling in order to show

47. Ellul, *On Freedom, Love, and Power*, 73.
48. Ellul, *Political Illusion*, 135.
49. Ellul, *Subversion*, 121.

himself as a stranger in this world all the more."[50] Martin Luther, he explained, returned to the world from the monastery "as a radical criticism and protest against the secularization of Christianity which had taken place within monasticism. By recalling the Christians into the world he called them paradoxically out of it all the more."[51]

In the case of Americanized Christians, and to borrow from the poet Wordsworth, "the world is too much with them." The problem is not so much that American Christians form political opinions and make political choices, but that they do so with little regard for Christ their model and the teachings they claim to follow and confess. They do interpretive violence to those very teachings and so distort the gospel, and they put their faith and hope in politicians and political parties rather than in God. Faithfulness to the word of God, Ellul writes, is "the essential work of the Church more than political or evangelical or moral action, etc."[52] As Whitehead and Perry observed, to fuse national identity with Christianity "destroys the witness of the kingdom of God."[53]

Although American Christians generally pride themselves on their knowledge of the Bible, they seem conveniently to have forgotten or ignored injunctions like those of the psalmist: "Do not put your trust in princes, in mortal men, who cannot save. When their spirit departs, they return to the ground; on that very day their plans come to nothing" (Ps 146:3–4). Instead, such Christians put their trust in a political party, in a particular administration and government, in America, in the state. Christians in America fail to remember that Jesus did not engage in or promote a politics of any kind. He did not call for the overthrow of the wicked, oppressive, profane, and worldly political power known as the Roman Empire. On the contrary, he embodied love and obedience to God, peace and good will to men.

---

50. Bonhoeffer, *Cost of Discipleship*, 297.
51. Bonhoeffer, *Cost of Discipleship*, 298.
52. Ellul, *Apocalypse*, 139.
53. Whitehead and Perry, *Taking America Back*, 163.

If we look first to Jesus, the prototype, our model, and to his example, we must acknowledge that he never sought to influence or change any government, not the Roman government or its secular society. He never allied himself in any way with any political power. When tempted by the devil in the wilderness, he rejected the offer to rule over all the kingdoms of the world (Matt 4:8–10). On the night of his arrest, Jesus made absolutely clear that his "kingdom is not of this world" (John 18:36). It is consequently demonstrably wrong for followers of Jesus to seek to make a national kingdom of Jesus in this world, not to mention this country. The only statement he made about government was: "Give back to Caesar what is Caesar's and to God what is God's" (Mark 12:17). It is a clear message to his followers to have nothing to do with the secular, political world and to be devoted instead to the kingdom of heaven. He never engaged in political discourse, never told his followers to lobby for anything like an end to abortion or the defense of reproductive rights, for a reduction or increase in taxes, or to champion or oppose homosexuality in the Roman world, a world defined by sensual pleasure, idolatry, violence, power, and political machinations. As Paul described that world in his Letter to the Romans, the people of Rome had become filled "with every kind of wickedness, evil, greed and depravity. They are full of envy, murder, strife, deceit and malice. They are gossips, slanderers, God-haters, insolent, arrogant and boastful; they invent ways of doing evil; they disobey their parents; they have no understanding, no fidelity, no love, no mercy" (Rom 1:29–32). Yet, Paul gave no instructions to try to change the Roman world by becoming involved with Roman politics. And the secular world he describes surely parallels our own.

Jesus did not preach about religious freedom or religious rights, which are the preoccupation of so many Christians today. He did not insist on prayer in public places, as does the Congressional Prayer Caucus Foundation, whose members advocate for "the right of individuals to engage in public prayer and the expression of faith in God."[54] Rather, Jesus told his followers to pray

54. Congressional Prayer Caucus Foundation, "About."

in secret (Matt 6:6). He did not seek or form alliances with the Roman governors or kings of the region in order to promote God's kingdom, as have so many religious leaders in America. He did not preach a message about the sanctity of private property or family or the military or free speech or the right to bear arms or free enterprise or some kind of independence from Rome. He did not commend the Essenes and praise their revolt with the Maccabees against the Syrians nor the Zealots who agitated to rebel against the Romans and drive them out of Judea. Indeed, one of the twelve disciples was a Zealot named Simon who abandoned the political movement to follow Jesus.

*maybe*

Jesus set us free from any and every political illusion. Granted, his teachings always had and still have social and economic repercussions, but only as lived out in love toward God and the neighbor who, as the parable of the Good Samaritan teaches (Luke 10:25–37), is the person we meet on our way in life, someone we might never have seen before and would not necessarily associate with, someone left at the side of the road, a stranger, a person in distress. Jesus did not expect or demand the pagan Roman world to behave like God's people—only his followers were commanded to live as he lived. Obedience to Jesus is for those who are his followers, not for those who are not. In his *Church Dogmatics*, Karl Barth wrote that "there can be no question of a general rule, a Christian system confronting that of the world, in competition with it, and in some way to be brought in harmony with it."[55]

In the rush to endorse what is labeled a conservative political agenda, Americanized Christians fail "to test the spirits to see whether they are from God," as 1 John 4:1 exhorts. For Christians, Scripture has always been acknowledged as authoritative and the standard by which to test and judge themselves and the world. But politics pushes the authority of the Bible aside. Passages like "do not steal, do not lie, do not deceive, do not defraud; do not pervert justice" from Leviticus (19:11ff); "There will always be poor people in the land. Therefore I command you to be openhanded toward your brothers and toward the poor and needy in your land;" "Do

55. Barth, *Church Dogmatics*, Vol. IV, Part 2, 550.

not deprive the alien or fatherless of justice" from Deuteronomy
(15:11 and 24:17); and "Love your enemies and pray for those who
persecute you, that you may be sons of your Father in heaven"
from Matthew (5:43–45) should, but do not, give Americanized
Christians pause and guidance in relation to the political realm.
Instead, troublesome policies and practices promoted by Rove,
Rice, Rumsfeld, Cheney, and Bush on the one hand, McConnell,
Pompeo, Pence, Barr, and Trump on the other carry the day with
Americanized Christians. Lies and false pretenses, the spread of
misinformation and disinformation, rulings to legitimate torture
of enemy combatants, military strikes with civilian casualties, the
separation of children from parents who entered the country il-
legally, the provocation of prejudice and violence, cronyism, or
manifest corruption have not changed the allegiance of Americanized Christians to the politicians who approved and employed such
tactics. Christians must first ask and endeavor to decide whether a
policy or action is *righteous*, that is, whether it is right in the eyes
of God.

In America, the church has adopted the values of the world,
of the nation-state. It endorses a politics of worldly success, economic prosperity, consumer capitalism, and patriotic nationalism.
Rather than seeking first the kingdom of God and his righteousness, Americanized Christians seek first the kingdom of this world,
of America. It is of course the responsibility of the church to represent and declare instead the values of Christ's kingdom, values
not of this world. As Rudolf Bultmann said, "it is not the effect that
it has on world history that legitimates the Christian faith, but its
strangeness within the world; and the strangeness is the bearing of
those whose love for each other is grounded in the divine love."[56]
When leading American Christians agree with reigning American politics, in other words, with the state, with the world, when
the Christian church becomes enamored of the world's ways and
means, of influence, violence, and power, then something is surely
wrong with the church. The failure of this Americanized Christianity to reject the world, the nation-state, America, is surely a

56. Bultmann, *Gospel of John*, 529.

betrayal of the church's calling. How can the church challenge the world and its ways if it has gone to bed with the world, if it has prostituted itself to the state?

The church, Ellul asserted, must be "the question that God puts to the world."[57] But it cannot do so when the church joins forces with the secular state, when the church adopts and accepts its secular agenda. Even Friedrich Nietzsche, that great critic of Christianity and the church, understood that challenge as its responsibility: "The purest and truest adherents to Christianity," he wrote, "have always questioned and restricted rather than promoted worldly success and so-called 'historical power.' . . . Expressed in Christian terms: the devil is the regent of the world and the master of successes and progress; he is the actual power in all historical powers, and that is how it will essentially remain—even though it will be downright painful to the ears of those who are accustomed to the deification of success and historical power."[58] The truth is painful indeed, but necessary.

When the church endorses and shares the values and politics of the world, of the US, it rejects God and becomes apostate. As Ellul and Crumb indicate, politics leads away and astray from God. The church has compromised itself and fails utterly when it accepts the offer of the state to be its ally, or when of its own accord it extends such an offer to the state. When it becomes American, the church is first corrupted, then bankrupted. Christians wrongly align themselves with patriotism and nationalism. They should know and confess that there is nothing sacred about the flag, the Pledge of Allegiance, the Declaration of Independence, or the US Constitution and its amendments.

The church cannot challenge the world—even and especially the political doctrines of the US—when it collaborates and colludes with the nation-state. In reference to the Sermon on the Mount and the famous passage redefining "an eye for an eye, and a tooth for a tooth" (Matt 5:38–42), Bonhoeffer reminds us that

57. Ellul, *Politics of God*, 142.

58. Nietzsche, *Vom Nutzen und Nachteil der Historie,* my translation, 368–69.

"This saying of Christ removes the Church from the sphere of politics and law. The church is not to be a national community like the Old Israel, but a community of believers without political or national ties."[59] According to Jesus, if someone strikes you, turn the other cheek; if someone takes your tunic, give him your cloak also; love your enemies and pray for those who persecute you (Matt 5). These radical teachings contradict everything the world and America holds near and dear, everything it considers normal and natural. As Kurt Vonnegut, the fourth-generation German-American religious skeptic, had one of his fictional characters ask, "what could be more un-American . . . than sounding like the Sermon on the Mount?"[60] An Americanized Christianity turns a deaf ear to Jesus' words.

Thanks to the liaison of church and state, Americanized Christians have been able to accept and condone self-interest, indifference, and apathy toward the downtrodden, and a persistent assertion of falsehood as truth. As Bonhoeffer observed, the Christian gives "visible proof of his calling" in opposition to such policies and practices. "Where the world seeks gain," he declared,

> the Christian will renounce it. Where the world exploits, he will dispossess himself, and where the world oppresses, he will stoop down and raise up the oppressed. If the world refuses justice, the Christian will pursue mercy, and if the world takes refuge in lies, he will open his mouth for the dumb, and bear witness to the truth.[61]

It is a great irony indeed that secularists often think, speak, and act more like Bonhoeffer, more like Christians should, than Americanized Christians do.

Christians are to put their trust and to hope *not* in politics, but in Jesus Christ alone. The Christian hope, Bonhoeffer underscores, "is not set on this world, but on Christ and his kingdom."[62] And as

---

59. Bonhoeffer, *Cost of Discipleship*, 157.

60. Vonnegut, *Hocus Pocus*, 97.

61. Bonhoeffer, *Cost of Discipleship*, 289.

62. Bonhoeffer, *Cost of Discipleship*, 291.

Ellul explains, the Christian hope "implies the total rejection of the confusion between the kingdom of God and any kind of politico-social system."[63] What is more, he argues, "to conceive that history ends inevitably and normally in the Kingdom, by technical progress or by political revolutions; to conceive that God acts in history by the intermediary of the political actions of man, revolutionary or conservative, is the complete opposite of hope."[64] That is, we have no need of God and no reason to hope in him, if we believe and expect politics to provide us with the answers and solutions we desire.

Americanized Christians have been seduced by worldly power, the power of their political parties (whichever they currently most favor), and the power of their nation-state. Yet, they do well to recall the temptation of Jesus in the desert. According to the Gospel of Matthew, the devil took Jesus up "to a very high mountain and showed him all the kingdoms of the world and their splendor. 'All this I will give to you,' he said, 'if you will bow down and worship me.'" Certainly, Christians remember what Jesus said in response: "Away from me, Satan! For it is written: 'Worship the Lord your God, and serve him only'" (Matt 4:8–10). For Americanized Christians, the temptation has been too great. The non-power lived out by Jesus Christ has proven inadequate and undesirable. It does not provide the tangible results they seek and want. Christian non-power looks like failure to the eyes of the world, but also to Americanized Christians. Even though Jesus discredited and defeated worldly power—"Fear not, for I have overcome the world," he told his disciples in the face of his arrest and crucifixion (John 16:33)—twenty-first-century Americanized Christians have embraced the very power their Christ overcame.

63. Ellul, *Apocalypse*, 59.
64. Ellul, *Apocalypse*, 62.

CHAPTER 2

# The Church and Technology

*Zillah also had a son, Tubal-Cain, who forged all kinds*
*of tools out of bronze and iron.*

—GENESIS 4:22

WHO CAN DENY THAT gasoline-, solar-, and battery-powered devices, not to mention cell phones, computers, and their extensions, structure our everyday existence? Who can deny that techniques orchestrate life today, whether in business, medicine, education, leisure activity, politics, or even the church? Technology is our catch-all term for this aspect of our lives. It is both the dominant feature and force in our lived experience. It is a total environment; we can even say it is our *reality*. We live and breathe *in*, but now also *for* it. And the most salient feature of technology today is the Internet.

As everyone must know, the Internet is awash with information. It is also generally acknowledged that such a condition is both good and desirable, but we would do well to think again about that attitude. We should not forget how Claude Shannon, a pioneer in computer technologies, first defined *information* as "any communicated message, regardless of its meaning."[1] Indeed,

1. As summarized by Woolley, *Virtual Worlds*, 69.

information, as James Gleick points out in his book on chaos theory, corresponds to "neither knowledge nor meaning. Its basic units were not ideas or concepts or even, necessarily, words or numbers. This thing could be sense or nonsense—but the engineers and mathematicians could measure it, transmit it, and test the transmission for accuracy."[2] Certainly, the vast array of computer-mediated messages communicated and streaming over the Internet give evidence of that undifferentiated confusion of sense and nonsense. Even so, the Internet has come to be regarded and to function as the key repository and source of information, now uncritically understood to be something invariably intelligible and meaningful. At the same time *information* subtly transformed into *knowledge*, and the Internet became the primary and all but sole source of knowledge, indeed, *all* knowledge. (Ask any of our high schoolers or college students or neighbors or even yourself, if anyone really has a different opinion.)

According to Hubert Dreyfus, "The Internet is not just a new technological innovation; it is a new *type* of technological innovation; one that brings out the very essence of technology."[3] If the essence of technology, he goes on to explain, "is to make everything easily accessible and optimizable, then the Internet is the perfect technological device."[4] We might say it epitomizes late-modern technology. Technology, and its current quintessence the Internet, now at our fingertips on the smartphones always with us, permeates every aspect of contemporary life. It consequently shapes, determines, and redefines religious life as well, and its effect is by no means subtle. It comes as no surprise then that pastors of Christian churches in the United States turn to the Internet for inspiration, for resources, for sermon material, even for entire, finished sermons. And parishioners or congregants in turn are treated to the fruits of such pastoral Internet browsing, research, or purchases. The technological component in a variety of forms is an unexamined, yet usually welcome addition to church life. What

2. Gleick, *Chaos*, 255.

3. Dreyfus, *On the Internet*, 1.

4. Dreyfus, *On the Internet*, 1–2.

I explore here first is how pastors and parishioners rely on technology, specifically the Internet, as a means to understand, define, and practice their religion. Second, I examine how the church typically engages with technology in general. This chapter asks and suggests responses to such questions as: What does it mean that preachers find "inspiration" on the Internet, and what does that mean for contemporary Christian life in the United States? How should the church address technology and our relationship with it? What should Christians say and do about this our undeniable current technological condition?

Already some years ago now, I heard a pastor begin a sermon with a telling remark that went something like this: "As I was doing research for my message this past week, I found some pertinent material on the Internet." I have to admit that for some time already my personal radar had been suspecting Internet sources for many of the sermon anecdotes and illustrations I had been hearing in church services, so I was especially interested in that pastor's remark. The pastor in question went on to explain what he had found, which was really only some engaging quotations pertinent to his theme, made by various famous persons. In addition, that service included an accompanying picture slideshow and Power-Point presentation that I suspect were part of a whole package and that I will discuss subsequently. What struck me as noteworthy was that the pastor used the Internet as a source of material for the sermon and probably the worship service as a whole. Granted, pastors could, before the advent of the Internet, avail themselves of various books written specifically to provide help for sermons. But the Internet takes such help to another level altogether. Quotations, anecdotes, and exemplary illustrations for sermons found on the Internet are only the tip of a remarkable iceberg, and icebergs, even metaphorical ones, present grave dangers to all kinds of navigation.

A cursory Internet search immediately reveals an abundance of easily and readily available material, from sermon helps and illustrations to whole sermons and an extensive array of other ancillary "resources" for pastors in the pulpit. Admittedly, many pastors might well deliver excellent sermons, if they read good ones authored by an inspired preacher and appropriate to the current needs of the congregation, but that is a matter for another study. I have not looked at the quality of the materials and sermons available on the Internet, but if the rest of the Internet, or what the comedian Al Franken has ironically called "the prestigious Internet"[5] is anything to go by, I do not have very high expectations for the Internet supply of sermons.

A relatively quick and short search of the Internet produced a number of results such as: sermonsearch.com, sermoncentral.com, eSermons.com (no longer a site, but now sermons.com exists), crosswalk.com, higherpraise.com, bible.org, sermonlinks.com, searchgodsword.org (no longer on the Internet in 2020, but my browser automatically redirected me in my search for it to biblestudytools.com), sermonsnet.com, sermonmall.com, preachingtoday.com (from the prominent and popular magazine *Christianity Today*, which at the time had a separate webpage as well called preachingtodaysermons.com), logos.com, and preachersgoldmine.com (no longer online), to name only a few.[6] There are certainly many, many more such sites available online today for both pastors and parishioners to peruse. Judging by the abundance of websites devoted to sermons for pastors (not to mention what are called "Christian living resources"), there must be high demand for them, and it must be a thriving business.

Sermonsnet was originally designed to serve a Baptist constituency, while Searchgodsword informed that it could help "jazz up" messages with "Sermon Jazzers" and could even supply "200 FREE 'full-text' Sunday Sermons" (almost two years' worth of sermons).[7] Sermonsnet offered what looked to be a sermon for every occasion. The website showed a bulleted list of available

5. Franken, *Lies*, 17.

6. The following information was retrieved originally from the websites discussed here on June 23, 2008, but most of them were still to be found on the Internet in the summer of 2020. In order to simplify subsequent references to them, I do not provide elaborate web addresses for those sites each time they are mentioned, since they are easily found using the names cited here.

7. http://www.searchgodsword.org.

materials including: expository sermons, topical sermons, seasonal sermons, series sermons, revival sermons, evangelistic sermons, soul-winning sermons, funeral sermons, Easter sermons, Christmas sermons, Thanksgiving sermons, New Testament sermons, and Old Testament sermons. Sermoncentral's site menu included a "pastor's resource kit" and options to search that site for both PowerPoint presentations and sermons one might want to use at the next worship service. While eSermons had "thousands of *professionally published* sermons" on offer, Preachersgoldmine promised "a monthly outline paper" for "324 preachable sermons."[8] It is noteworthy that potential customers should be assured the sermons are not unpreachable. The subheading at the Preachingtoday webpage was "Be Inspired" with the implication that inspiration can be found and retrieved online.[9] At Logos, users can access Bible Software, which offers to read "all your books instantly, delivering just what you need at each step in your Bible study."[10] But how could an algorithm know what a pastor needed from all those books? One could also have sermons by such well-known names as Mike Huckabee, Bill Hybels, Rob Bell, and Rick Warren (all at Preachingtodaysermons) or Max Lucado, Charles Swindoll, and Jerry Falwell (at Sermoncentral).

Many of these resources come at a price, and most of these sermons are available through subscription. For Preachersgoldmine, it was $25 a year; for Sermoncentral $119.50 a year. For eSermons, there were various options starting at $64.95 a year for a package including "Sermons, Illustrations, Eulogies, Commentaries, & Dictionary" with an extra $29.95 each for worship and bulletin aids, dramas, and children's sermons. Sermonmall charged $49.95 a year, while a year's membership at Preachingtoday cost $69.95 and provided such help as "series builders, full sermon outlines and transcripts by many of today's best communicators and thousands of title suggestions." *Christianity Today*'s Preachingtodaysermons offered regularly priced Sermon Packs ranging

8. http://www.preachersgoldmine.com.
9. http://www.preachingtoday.com.
10. https://www.logos.com.

from $7.90 (for two) up to $51.35 (for thirteen), not to mention individual sermons like Rob Bell's "The Flames of Heaven" or Mike Huckabee's "Practice of Patience" for $4.95 each. On its FAQ page, Preachingtodaysermons announced that "Shopping at Preaching-TodaySermons is designed to be fun and easy!" Similarly, Preachersgoldmine stated that its sermon outlines were "designed to be a time saver," a service technology always promises. In addition, the Preachingtodaysermons website had a page with helpful hints like "How to Use Other People's Sermons with Integrity," which would not be necessary, if there were not some concern about the use of such materials.[11] Without doubt, such readily available Internet resources are only in such supply because there is a corresponding demand for them. Likewise, the whole Internet sermon enterprise/ industry appears to be very much devoted to the generation of income. Most troubling is that such sites encourage quick fixes and suggest that there is no need to spend time in prayer and reflection, which would otherwise be the inspiration and foundation necessary for any sermon as God's word for believers. Perhaps such online resources are for pastors who do not wish to spend time in prayer and reflection for inspiration.

Another popular and successful venture is Life.Church (previously known as Lifechurch.tv) founded by millionaire Craig Groeschel. Life.Church is a so-called multi-site church which comprises several campuses across the country: "one church meeting in multiple locations."[12] It manages this domain by using and relying on video and satellite technologies, so that what Dreyfus calls *telepresence* necessarily plays a major and pivotal role in that ministry. *Presence* has long been an essential of primary importance to Christians, whether it be the *presence of the Lord, presence of the kingdom,* or *real presence* in the Eucharist. Telepresence consequently represents a fundamental problem, for the most part unacknowledged or ignored, because there is no embodied presence in an actual physical environment when online. Especially

11. This information was collected from these websites in 2008.
12. https://www.life.church/.

problematic, as Dreyfus notes, it prevents "direct contact with reality."[13]

What Dreyfus observes about the professor in a telelecture applies also to the pastor in a telesermon: they are both "a prisoner of the camera operator and the sound engineer."[14] The person who telepreaches cannot directly interact with, respond to, or adjust to his or her distance-audience, and that audience need be no more engaged with the telepresent pastor than with anyone or anything in any other online activity. The computer, tablet, or smartphone we use always tempts us to check some other link or social network site while online. The technology always mediates, always erects an unrecognized barrier, always stands between preacher and audience, and always demands attention for itself. George Steiner alerts us to additional problems when he contrasts "real presence," where words have meaning and stand in relation to reality, with the cynical notion of "real absence," where "the truth of the word is in the absence of the world,"[15] that is, words have no actual relation to reality. Certainly the truth of the telesermon must then be in the absence of the world, since it occurs in cyberspace. Most troubling is the danger to the word and Word in such absent "presence."

Like other sites serving Christian customers, the Life.Church website (open.life.church) offered many and varied options and materials. On that site under *Resources*, the menu listed several choices, two especially germane to the present considerations: one labeled *Message Series*, the other *Message Topic*. The *Message Series* web page presented more than fifty different selections each with a brief and catchy abstract describing a topic. In 2008, many of the messages were devoted to sex (some salacious titles were: "Porn Sunday," "Satan's Sex Ed," "Goin' All the Way," "God Loves Sex," and "The Sex Files"). About as many other topics tended to fall into the self-help-through-positive-thinking category (titles

13. Dreyfus, *On the Internet*, 54.

14. Dreyfus, *On the Internet*, 64.

15. Steiner, *Real Presences*, 96.

included: "Parenthood," "Baggage," "Difficult People," "Life Development Plan," "Fear," and so on).[16]

I picked and clicked on one of the possibilities entitled "TXT" which was a three-week series about the Bible. For that series, Life. Church provided several other accessory materials: (1) a graphic for the church bulletin; (2) an invitation to insert and include in the bulletin; (3) a loop video that can be displayed on screen during the message, behind the speaker or pastor, to help "theme" the environment; (4) a video to open the series; and (5) what it called a "tease" video for each week, which could be used to arouse interest in the next message. Another mouse-click on Week 3 of the "TXT" series indicated that I could get (1) a message DVD, (2) a message outline for people to follow along with the teaching, (3) a message transcript with a word-for-word transcription of a single message, and (4) a set of small group questions. It was unclear whether the so-called *Message Series* was geared to an actual sermon series, a church education program, or both. In any case, I have experienced something very much like that package in several church services in different cities, where, as mentioned above, the message was accompanied by picture and PowerPoint slides on a large screen behind the pastor that *themed* the church service environment. Now Life.Church offers an app called "Church Metrics" which tracks and compiles data about church growth, "attendance, salvations, and more." But how can eternal salvation be calculated or even ascertained by an app, let alone another human being?

As often as not, Internet resources and materials for pastors and churches are, as noted, available for a price. Not to be left behind (pun intended) in the adoption and adaptation of new technologies for its subscribers and constituencies, *Christianity Today*, generally highly regarded in the Christian community, apparently attempts to live up to its label in the age of the Internet as Christianity for *today* with a website and web pages for much more than its periodical. At the Preachingtoday site, one finds the following enticement : "If you sign up for a premium membership, you'll

16. Although these headings and topics were found on the website in 2008, the same or similar material was available in 2020.

have over 8,000 sermon illustrations."[17] In 2020, there were three options and plans with "pricing to fit your budget": a monthly subscription for $4, an annual for $99, and a two year for $169.[18]

Memberships or subscriptions that come at a price, in fact, a premium, whether literal or figurative, give pause for thought. Many Internet resource sites for pastors and churches, like so much else on the Internet, come at a cost. But what cost? Might the price be too high? Might the price be a deal with a devil of sorts, a Faustian bargain that requires the soul as collateral? What happens to churches and pastors and Christian religious life, when those involved rely increasingly, maybe predominantly, on such Internet sources and resources? My sense, and fear, is that religious life changes not for the better, but for the worse, when the Internet becomes not only the *default*, but the *first* source to turn to for something so important to Christian religious life, to the worship service, and to the sermon, typically the vehicle for what Christians consider the word of God for their lives. When the Internet becomes the source of materials, of knowledge, of "inspiration" for the church, religious life begins to dilute, to fade, to deteriorate.

When worship services and sermons can be had as prefab packages, when pastors can get and employ preselected illustrations, not to mention whole ready-to-preach sermons, then the food for religious life resembles all the other packaged, processed foods on the shelves of our supermarkets. It is no longer food, but a food-like substance, a far cry from real food. In the same way processed food lacks substance and even proves harmful to physical health, so too prepackaged, processed sermons lack substance and prove harmful to religious and spiritual health. The worship service takes on a phony and artificial character. Certainly, the sermon is sullied, and the word becomes wooden. One would be hard-pressed to find inspiration and profound meaning in such a message, let alone spiritual nourishment and sustenance.

17. Again, this information was originally collected from the website in question in 2008.

18. https://www.preachingtoday.com.

What lurks inside the preaching of a sermon downloaded, and often purchased, from the Internet is a fundamental dishonesty as well. Granted, my experience is limited, but in spite of tips about how to use such sermons with integrity, I have yet to hear a pastor say: "I bought this sermon on the Internet" or "Today's service makes use of a package of materials taken from such and such Internet site." Is it simply the quick-and-easy fix for a pastor who has too little time or no inclination to prepare a sermon and service through study, reflection, prayer, and meditation, once the essential ingredients for a message understood to be the word of God for the lives of believers? For that matter, how can a ready-to-serve Internet sermon truly speak to a specific, local congregation with its own particular problems and needs? Even if made to order (like the papers students can buy over the Internet and hand in for their coursework), such sermons written by anonymous strangers can hardly qualify as honest and sincere.

The user-friendly Internet sermon caters to customers and conforms to the marketplace. What that means for sermons and religious life is unsettling as well. As John MacArthur observed about megachurch theology in general, "salesmanship requires that negative subjects like divine wrath be avoided. Consumer satisfaction means that the standard of righteousness cannot be raised too high. The seeds of a watered-down Gospel are thus sown in the very philosophy that drives many ministries today."[19] Without doubt, his criticisms would aptly describe a sermon taken from an Internet site. After all, the prefab, Internet sermon must necessarily remain generic and strive for the lowest common denominator in order to appeal to the largest and broadest demographic possible. One size has to fit, if not all, at least as many as possible. Prepackaged Internet sermons inevitably lack vitality, cease to inspire, and turn insipid. And so does religious life as a whole. Of course, great sermons with broad applicability exist and deserve to be widely disseminated, read, and heard. But something else is also at stake when Internet sites market and sell sermons. "Money changers" have, so to speak, set up their tables in "the temple."

19. As quoted by Fitzgerald, "Come One, Come All," 55.

36

When churches market and brand themselves in the image of consumer capitalism, when sermons themselves become a marketable product, a product which can be had for a price, the content of sermons and of religious life necessarily changes and suffers. It becomes adapted to and reflects its source, in this case, the Internet. If Marshall McLuhan"s famous dictum asserted over fifty years ago in *Understanding Media* still holds today, and I believe it does, that "the medium is the message,"[20] then the message of the Internet sermon is the Internet or technology in general, since the Internet is now the chief embodiment of technology. In addition, McLuhan understood that "the formative powers in the media are the media themselves."[21] Hence, the formative power of the sermon available on and from the Internet is *not* the content of the particular sermon per se, but rather that of the Internet.

Given our current devotion and relation to technology, there must be, in all likelihood even implicitly, the sense that the sermon taken from the Internet must be inherently better, because it has been found, retrieved, and received from the computer, from the Internet, from the beneficent hand of technology (almost like divine inspiration or revelation of the past—and in spite of the minds and hands that actually supplied the sermons to the websites in the first place).

The word *religion* originates in the Latin language. Its root *ligare* means "to bind," its prefix *re-* "back," hence *to bind back*. The idea of binding oneself or being bound back to someone or something in the word *religion* takes on a new and ominous significance when linked with the Internet or the World Wide Web. In their abbreviated forms, the Net or the Web subtly, and surreptitiously, reveal an essential characteristic. Nets and webs ensnare, capture, and hold prey. Like religion, the Internet or the World Wide Web binds us back to itself. In the same way, the Net or Web now replaces religion as our source of knowledge, inspiration, and meaning. Even though we know or learn to beware of Internet sites and sources, to question the validity of information retrieved and

20. McLuhan, *Understanding Media*, 7.
21. McLuhan, *Understanding Media*, 21.

received from such sites and sources, we still turn to the Internet and depend on its plenitude of information, if not grace.

Often enough, we hear the church explain, using the same arguments the world uses, that technology is not a problem as long as it is used right. However, as Jacques Ellul pointed out, new technology is typically and "necessarily used as soon as it is available, without distinction of good or evil."[22] We do not really make conscious decisions about whether or not to use the available technologies, nor do we really have a choice about how to use the technology, since its use is predetermined by its fundamental design. Technologies function as they are devised—hammers hammer, saws saw, computers compute, knives cut, guns shoot bullets, automobiles transport people and hurtle down highways, televisions are made for watching, and so on—but also not as intended or expected. For example, knives and guns can be used to injure and kill other living beings. Automobiles are involved in minor and major accidents, causing injury and death. What is more, they contribute an enormous amount to environmental pollution. Television trivializes and turns everything it broadcasts, whether educational or political content, pleasant or unpleasant news, peace or war, humorous or serious programs, into mere entertainments (see Neil Postman, *Amusing Ourselves to Death: Public Discourse in the Age of Showbusiness*). Social media both connects and disconnects people, indeed, may disconnect individuals even more than it connects them. Many studies have demonstrated that our current devotion to and use of digital devices and media has not liberated us as much as increased our fear, paranoia, and isolation (see, for instance, Sherry Turkle, *Alone Together: Why We Expect More from Technology and Less from Each Other*). Amazon and Google provide truly astonishing assistance and possibility, but also openly and surreptitiously collect information on (un)witting users that those companies then use in whatever ways they choose. Technology succeeds and fails, not because it is used correctly or incorrectly, but because its failures are co-extant with its successes. The two cannot be separated from each other. There is no such

22. Ellul, *Technological Society*, 99.

thing as a neutral technology whose good or evil depends on how it is used. Technology in fact erases the distinctions between good and evil, true or false, natural and artificial, real and simulated. As Marshall McLuhan observed, "Our conventional response to all media, namely that it is how they are used that counts, is the numb stance of the technological idiot."[23]

Nor can the church argue that technology can as it were be "baptized" for our use, in other words, be brought under control and made acceptable for use by Christians. As with the idea of proper and improper use, this reasoning is false. Technology today is unlike technology at any other time in human history: It resists any such "baptism," transformation, or control. It is not merely a question of machines or digital devices, what we can call material technology (tools, artifacts, and mechanisms), but of nonmaterial technology as well (methods, procedures, and strategies), in a word, *techniques* used to engineer and program individuals and society, from students in school and employees at work, to commerce, the environment, and human health. Everything, every situation, and everyone becomes something to be controlled and optimized, made to operate like a machine, all in the service of efficiency and utility. While there may seem to be many, separate, individual technologies in our world today, they actually constitute a vast ensemble of innumerable, interconnected technologies that combine to form one great, unified system. In Ellul's judgement, technology "is not a collection of technical goods which may be freely used, but a total ideological and pragmatic system which imposes structures, institutions, and modes of behavior on all members of society."[24] As an all-encompassing system, technology is now utterly beyond our control. Far from transforming technology as we would wish it to be, it transforms us, making us over in its own image, ultimately to the point of dehumanizing us who are made in the image of God.

Although technology includes techniques as well as devices, most people today primarily think of technology as those things

23. McLuhan, *Understanding Media*, 18.

24. Ellul, *Ethics of Freedom*, 310.

connected to the digital universe. In consequence, I restrict my comments here chiefly to such examples. *The Washington Post* reported that in 2019, on average, "American eight-to-twelve-year-olds spent four hours and forty-four minutes on screen media each day. And teens average seven hours and twenty-two minutes—not including time spent using screens for school or homework." The average time kids spend watching online videos has doubled in four years.[25] *PC Magazine* similarly reported that the average adult spent 5.9 hours per day with digital media in 2018.[26] During the coronavirus pandemic of 2020, with children as it were "going to school online" and countless adults working remotely from home, those numbers have undoubtedly increased significantly.

How different are we Christians in our use of and devotion to technology? Most of us own and employ all the various technologies everyone else does. We and our children spend hours each day with our screens—at school, at work, at home. The vast majority of us, our friends, and our families, have and regularly use and have become dependent on, even enslaved to, automobiles, smartphones, PCs, TVs, video game consoles, and so on. Like so many others, we Christians devote hours to Facebook, email, Twitter, Instagram, digital games, YouTube, Google, Amazon, and texting, not to mention the myriad other technological interactions now on offer. Like everyone else, we Christians sit next to or across from each other, but pay more attention to our smartphones than to the other person(s) there present (but absent) with us. And we do so with little or no thought to whether we should do so or not. We even make excuses for doing so.

The church is certainly not to be anti-technology, but it must speak to the place and role of technology in our lives, in the lives of individual believers, and in the corporate life of the church, especially in an age when technology has such dominance and power. Along with many others, I have argued that technological idealism (or utopianism) is the dominant ideology of the world today (see my *Narratives of Technology*). It is hardly an exaggeration to

25. Siegel, "Tweens, teens and screens."
26. Marvin, "Tech Addiction."

say that the world loves, even worships technology. As Ellul observed, "The real religion of our times [is] the dominant forces of the technological society,"[27] and the dominant expression of those forces and that society is now the Internet. The world believes in continuous technological progress, ultimately resulting in a new idyllic existence. In this belief system, technology will solve all our problems, eliminate our woes, heal our iniquities, and cure our diseases. The world sees technology perform miracles: the blind receive their sight, the lame walk, the mute speak, the hopeless at last have hope. Its blessings for humanity seem to be without number and new every day.

In the world's view, technology enhances our existence and makes life ever better. It is the bearer of all good gifts: it gives us our crops, our health, our jobs, our shelter. It promises us ease, convenience, and comfort, but above all, technology increases our freedom and power. In this worldview, technology becomes the machine of inevitable progress and unlimited possibility, of the advance and improvement of all conditions: mechanical and organic, material and psychological, physical and spiritual. As the world sees it, technology offers otherwise unattainable knowledge; it represents the source of new, fabulous powers; it bestows gifts upon humanity and remedies the ills of society; it unites us with one another; indeed, it *perfects* the world *and* humanity. Whether in matters of health, environment, or prosperity, "salvation" is not really expected from Jesus Christ, but from technology. How different really are the beliefs of Christians from everyone else about technology?

Like God, technology is glorious. Like God, it is incomprehensible and impossible to master. Like God, it appears to be omnipresent, omniscient, and omnipotent, especially as embodied in the Internet/World Wide Web. Last, but certainly not least, we seek help and rely on it for anything and everything we might need.[28] Revelation and inspiration come not from God, but from technology, especially from the computer and all its appendages, from the

27. Ellul, *Technological Society*, 418.
28. Cf. Ellul, *Technological Bluff*, 346.

Internet. But the church knows that technology is not God. The church has a duty to expose and reject such beliefs as false.

Amazon, Google, Facebook, and Microsoft are massive monopolies of products, services, information, and more. While the pretext is that they provide us with countless benefits, the harm they do is largely ignored. At one time, "don't be evil" with its subtle religious overtones was Google's unofficial motto and was included in its corporate code of conduct. Google's parent company Alphabet has now repackaged that directive (or reminder) as "do the right thing." Both sound noble, but really express something innocuous, and actually mask whatever questionable practices Alphabet and its subsidiaries engage in. One of those subsidiaries, YouTube, is "notorious for pushing users toward . . . conspiracy theory videos, as a consequence of the most common user choices on the site and how the platform's predictive algorithms are written."[29] But conspiracy theories present fantasies and outright lies as truth. Seemingly benevolent, Google stands accused of helping countries such as China repress political dissent. Besides handling or using posted data in highly questionable ways, Facebook has permitted content which ranges from hate speech and mis- and disinformation to the incitement of violence and criminal activity. How and when has the church addressed such issues as they relate to Christians?

The domination of technology in the world today leads or even compels the church to adopt and adapt to, in ever greater measure, whatever technology has to offer. Certainly, the prevalence of technology in the church varies from denomination to denomination and congregation to congregation, even individual to individual. Some have likely maintained a healthy distance from technology, while others have welcomed it, even wholeheartedly, into their lives and into the worship service itself. Most church communities have asserted that they need to change with the times, to adopt new technologies as they emerge in order to keep pace with the changing attitudes and behaviors of their congregations. They want to be "relevant." I cannot think of or cite any Old Testament or New Testament efforts to be "relevant," however. Church

29. McNeil, "Search and Destroy," 14.

leaders maintain that they are responding to what they perceive the members of their churches need and want. And they argue that by employing popular technologies as they become available, they either retain members or draw in new believers and members. A Christian friend of mine and a leader in his church community informed me that his church has had a Facebook account for several years. Recently, his church launched a Twitter account. In each case, his church community never paused to think about or analyze these decisions. Rather, it adopted those technologies without a second thought, without thinking about the pros and cons of using Facebook and Twitter, without evaluating them and their effects. Such choices and actions are typical. No one brought attention to Facebook policies about content or (so-called) privacy. No one noted that Facebook uses the data from all its subscribers to fashion a platform that manipulates and controls users. No one paused to point out that Twitter spreads inanity and triviality as well as rumor, falsehood, and malice, perhaps to a greater extent than content with substance, truth, and integrity.

It is not unusual for churches to employ a technology without examining or understanding it, neither how it functions nor what deficiencies or deleterious effects it has. For example, a great many congregations have for some time already adopted PowerPoint for worship services, but without first considering the defects along with the perceived benefits of that technology. Little if any critical thought can have gone into such choices. In the world, PowerPoint has become ubiquitous and the preferred mode of presentation for anything and everything. The church, too, has found a use for it. Following practices in the world of business and education, the church sees PowerPoint as the new, "cool" model for delivery of its hymns, sermons, and various other complementary materials. But it has failed to recognize how that technology alters and diminishes content. Computer projectors and big screens are now a part of a great many church services. Song lyrics, Bible verses, pictures, and sermon content appear as PowerPoint displays at the front of church sanctuaries/auditoriums. Critics like Edward Tufte have pointed out serious problems with PowerPoint, however (see his *The Cognitive Style of PowerPoint*). PowerPoint restricts and minimizes content. It focuses attention not on the words and Word spoken by the preacher, but on a few phrases (ideally following the 6x6 rule: no more than six bullet points with six words each per slide) and on images on the screen that distract the audience and work against concentration. PowerPoint presentations diminish and trivialize the content of the message to the point of meaninglessness. Worst of all, PowerPoint devalues the word, in this case, God's Word for our lives, since it transforms the message into bits and pieces like sound bites and with the addition of pictures to make the presentation more "interesting" or appealing, the visual takes precedence over the spoken Word. Finally, PowerPoint transforms everything into entertainment, hardly something a church service should be.

Of late, especially in response to the coronavirus pandemic as it spread around the world in 2020, countless churches resorted to church online, either livestreaming or using something like Zoom for meetings and worship services. With gathering together inside a church building inadvisable, such modes and means of communicating with the members of the church may be the only option, but the members are still separated and isolated from each other. A meeting with the minister of the Word and the other participants, each in a small rectangle on the computer screen, leaves much to be desired. We may see and hear each other, but we are not truly together. Something artificial informs the online presence which is of course at core an absence, as Steiner asserted. In addition, we become viewers much the same as when we watch television or movies. We are more spectator than participant. Granted, a pandemic does not afford many other options, but we must be cognizant of what we lose when we transfer religious life to Internet connections. While we may take advantage of and find some benefit in such online interaction, we should acknowledge the defects. The unavoidable distortions, glitches, and delays interrupt and diminish the experience. Moreover, whatever kind of platform we use for Internet communications suffers from one significant flaw: a technology like Zoom or Skype cannot truly accommodate the multidimensionality of humans present together and necessary for full human interaction. Every exchange is a one-way street, every view is tunnel vision, because of the technology. It does not allow us to blend words and thoughts as a real, true assembly of living, breathing people. To "pass the peace" online cannot begin to approach or accomplish what occurs when people are physically together, face to face, among a host of others doing the same.

In *Religion And Technology in the 21st Century: Faith in the E-world*, Susan E. George presents a collection of information about the possibilities of church online: "what is church, what is a community, what is an acceptable type of 'presence' in order for there to be authentic corporate life, and other such questions surrounding a religious use of technology."[30] For the most part, she simply reports or presents typologies based on the findings of various studies and surveys. For example, she observes:

> The "meeting together" that is important in Christian communities includes this depth of encounter that the enhanced social presence of virtual worlds brings. However, the absence of physical presences creates a barrier for many religiously minded. Whether sophisticated virtual environments would ever alleviate the "lack of signal" in physical presence remains to be seen.[31]

While she admits certain difficulties, drawbacks, or even flaws with the church's use of technology, she inclines to the view that "technology may be creating a more authentic expression of religion through virtual communities that enhance aspects of human interrelation over face-to-face contact,"[32] even that technology may promote the transcendence that religious practice has sought and taught.[33] All in all, George fails to examine the church's use of technology in any very critical way. Rather, she presents variations of how religion has appropriated certain technologies, in particular, the Internet and AI for online and virtual interaction.

30. George, *Religion and Technology*, 176.
31. George, *Religion and Technology*, 176.
32. George, *Religion and Technology*, 253.
33. Cf. George, *Religion and Technology*, 254.

She comments on assorted versions of Internet church and virtual church, but neglects the adverse features of such versions of "church."

A final example illustrates the failure to make a critical assessment of technology and the church's adoption of it. In the summer of 2020, in the midst of the coronavirus pandemic, when church communities and organizations were struggling with doors closed for worship services and turning to Zoom and online streaming, a denomination with which I have been affiliated (the Christian Reformed Church) published three short pieces about technology in its official magazine *The Banner*: "Living Out Our Faith in a Technological World," by Brian Clark and Matt Kuzcinski, "Using Technology to Support Worship Leaders," by Joyce Borger, and "Technology: A Reality and a Gift," by Colin P. Watson Sr. The articles all sing the praises of technology. They describe how technology has proven wonderfully advantageous and afforded special means to allow for meetings, to facilitate devotions, or other "connections." As noted above, technology undeniably offers us great advantages, but it also and always brings with it unavoidable disadvantages. In other words, technology is at all times and in all circumstances both a blessing and a curse. None of these three authors examine technology critically; they do not take the curses into account along with the blessings. In fact, one of the pieces begins with three objections to technology, only to reject each one as invalid. These three authors reveal once again the church's failure to engage in any careful reflection about or examination of technology before adopting and using it.

The church preaches and teaches that Christians are to be in, but not of the world, but as the church too readily conforms to the world and to technology, the people of the *Book* (the *biblia*) and the *Word* (the *logos*) too easily become a people of technology instead. We Christians must ask and identify in what, or better, in whom we put our faith. Of course, when confronted with such a question, we all answer: in God! We must likewise ask what or whom it is we serve? Again, we answer: God! But how honest are those answers? At the end of *The Technological System*, Ellul concluded that "the human being who uses technology today is by that very fact the human being who serves it."[34] The comment casts light on what may well be most troubling about the intersection of Christian life and technology.

If we wish to determine what a particular person or society holds sacred and values above all else, we need to identify what he or she or they most think about, pay attention to, and devote their time and lives to. There can be no doubt that technology with all its expressions, but especially the personal computer and Internet, have now become *sacred*. Just try to take away someone's smartphone or something now as ordinary as a television, and see what resistance and ire result. Citizens of the technological society cannot, must not, and dare not criticize technology which by definition is its very foundation, is necessarily its most important and revered possession, indeed, its *summum bonum* and most sacred reality. To do so would be, in effect, to blaspheme. But the sacralization of technology is the true blasphemy, as the church must acknowledge and admit. Its task is then to contest faith and devotion to the technological system.

If technology takes up so much of our time, if it occupies so many of our thoughts, if it commands such a place of importance in our lives, if it commands our attention (even obedience), it vies with our allegiance to God, indeed, it displaces God in our lives. It is a power and dominion at odds with the command to have no other gods before our God, the only God. It is a false god, an idol, and must be exposed and rejected as such. It must be stripped of its power over us. Do we seek first the kingdom of God or the kingdom of technology?

The world loves technology with heart, soul, strength, and mind. It cannot wait for the next smartphone, television, laptop, tablet, program, game, or app. The world spends its hours and days on screens, texting, tweeting, emailing, and surfing the Web. Does the church, do Christians, behave any different? Do we not live almost entirely as the world lives in relation to technology? How have we limited our use of technology: of automobiles, televisions,

34. Ellul, *Technological System*, 325.

PCs, smartphones, or of techniques for management, education, and relationships? We stand convicted. In recent decades, the church has had little or nothing to say about technology, except to follow the rest of the world and embrace it with more or less open arms. However, the church must lead, not follow the world. If the church is to be the word and the light to a world in ignorance and darkness, if it is to expose the ideologies of the world as false, it must challenge the faith the world, and the church, has in technology.

The twenty-first-century Christian church forgets or ignores its ancient mandate and fundamental obligation to challenge and reject the world that now leads a life governed and shaped by technology, a life that conforms to the values of technology. In its embrace of technology, arguing that it must do so to reach a twenty-first-century, technological society, must "meet people where they are," the church relinquishes its obligation to confront, unmask, and deny the world and its values. Instead of challenging technology, the church harmonizes with it. As Ellul points out, "It was formerly believed that technique and religion were in opposition and represented two totally different dispensations."[35] Of course, that opposition has disappeared, and there is now only one dispensation, to appropriate that old theological term: it is that of technology. The church, Ellul asserts in *The Politics of God and the Politics of Man*, must be "the question that God puts to the world,"[36] but the church cannot be such a question when it participates in the great celebration and festival of technology.

In *Works of Love*, Søren Kierkegaard asked: "If it is true, then, that all of secular life, its pomp, its diversion, its charms, can in so many ways imprison and ensnare a man, what is the earnest thing to do . . . ?"[37] In precisely that way, technology—the preeminent facet of secular life today—has captivated us *and* taken us captive. It has caught us as in its web or net and holds us fast. Kierkegaard posits two possible answers to his question: "either from sheer

---

35. Ellul, *Technological Society*, 423.
36. Ellul, *Politics of God*, 142.
37. Kierkegaard, *Works of Love*, 62.

earnestness to be silent in the church about things, or earnestly to speak about them there in order, if possible, to fortify men against the dangers of the world."[38] But there is really only one answer and course of action, as he concludes: "to talk about things of the world in a solemn and truly earnest manner."[39] So it is with technology. The church is to speak out seriously and emphatically about those things of the world, specifically technology that both enchants and entraps us, distracts us and leads us away from faith and hope in God.

As Hubert Dreyfus recognized, Kierkegaard understood true religious life, specifically true Christianity based on the incarnation, as "an unconditional commitment to something finite, and having the faith-given courage to take the risks required by such a commitment. Such committed life gives one a meaningful life in this world."[40] For Kierkegaard, such a committed and meaningful existence could only be realized within the religious, or spiritual, sphere. Arguing from Kierkegaard's attack on the mid-nineteenth-century press, Dreyfus concluded that today the Internet is "the ultimate enemy of unconditional commitment, but only the unconditional commitment of what Kierkegaard calls the religious sphere of existence can save us from the nihilistic leveling launched by the Enlightenment, promoted by the press and the public sphere, and perfected in the World Wide Web."[41] Sobering words of warning for a church that relies more and more on the Internet and all its attendant trappings. Ultimately, Dreyfus reminds us, the Internet promotes the demise and elimination of meaning.[42] What could be worse for a church, for the body of believers, which ostensibly exists to point to the source of all meaning?

The church and individual Christians must then lay bare the true nature of and forsake the false values and meaning offered by technology. We must curtail our use of technology, even renounce

---

38. Kierkegaard, *Works of Love*, 62.
39. Kierkegaard, *Works of Love*, 62.
40. Dreyfus, *On the Internet*, 122n42.
41. Dreyfus, *On the Internet*, 89.
42. Dreyfus, *On the Internet*, 102.

the technologies we love most. As technology erases all boundaries, it promises a life without limits, where everything is possible and permissible. To expect or live such a life is an act of rebellion against God. It is to commit the original sin again, the sin to want to know what God knows, indeed, to want to be God. We must acknowledge our apostasy, turn away from our love of technology, and turn our love back to God. Let Christians live out lives of faith, hope, and love, not in technology, but in God.

# PART II

*The World as Church*

CHAPTER 3

# Personal Religion

*I perceive that in every way you are very religious.*

—ACTS 17:22

## Religious Ambiguity

LONG-STANDING DEBATES ABOUT WHETHER America is a post-Christian society or a secular society are often confusing because the participants are not always clear about whether their pronouncements are meant to be factual or normative. In his 1961 book *The Death of God*, Gabriel Vahanian called America post-Christian. He meant, among other things, that Christianity had been absorbed by the larger culture, and while ostensibly alive and vibrant, was now in the service of a religiosity that by itself had nothing to do with Christianity. This was an immanentist religiosity that made a god of the human. God becomes an idealized man, but only a man, as in *Godspell*. Christianity here is a means to the end of human fulfillment and happiness. Vahanian refers to this form of Christianity as secularism.[1] The content of Christianity

---

1. Vahanian, *Death of God*.

53

has been emptied of its warnings about the world. In secularism Christianity signs a truce with the world.

For others the idea of America being a secular society meant identifying religion with Christianity, so that with the decline of Christianity, America was becoming nonreligious. Vahanian, however, is describing a gradual takeover of Christianity by humanism, which allowed the former to retain its identity. For him humanism was not secular but religious.

Prior to Vahanian's analysis, others made similar observations about religious change in the nineteenth century. In writing about religion in America, Alexis de Tocqueville asserted that Christianity was strong in America because public opinion favored it. Indeed, he proclaimed that public opinion was a kind of religion with the majority its prophet. In a democracy, he argued, the majority identified with the power of government. This was an early form of nationalism, a political religion.[2] Writing about the same time, Kierkegaard maintained that in Christendom, Christianity had been reduced to a "quack doctor," offering well-being, health, and happiness to the bourgeois Christian.[3] In both instances Christianity had been reduced to a means to meet societal or individual ends.

The best description of religious syncretism in America is Will Herberg's 1955 book *Protestant, Catholic, Jew.*[4] He maintained that the effective religion of Americans was the American Way of Life, which contained both personal and civic (political) religions. The main emphasis of the American Way of Life was psychological technique to help one achieve "peace of mind," whereby anxiety had been allayed and happiness achieved. Health, happiness, and success were interrelated components of this personal religion. The civic form of the American Way of Life entailed a belief in the sanctity of American democracy and its necessary ally, American capitalism, in short, America itself. The two forms of religion, personal and civic, were not in conflict because Americans believed

2. Tocqueville, *Democracy in America.*
3. Kierkegaard, *For Self-Examination.*
4. Herberg, *Protestant, Catholic, Jew.*

that democratic capitalism existed to advance the goals of the individual—health, happiness, success, peace of mind. Herberg waited until the final chapter to indicate his own position on the American Way of Life. He said unequivocally that Judaism and Christianity were opposed (or should be) to the American Way of Life and that they were never intended to be a means to achieve individual and societal goals. Protestantism, Catholicism, and Judaism had become denominations within the larger and more important religion, the American Way of Life. Devotion to the American Way of Life was idolatry!

Herberg's analysis indicates the difficulty in naming a religious phenomenon religious syncretism. For many conservative Christians, Christianity should be supportive of nationalism and capitalism. In this view it would be wrong not to bring Christianity into alignment with American democracy and American capitalism. Syncretism is in the eye of the beholder.

After Herberg, scholars have tended to emphasize either personal religion or civic religion, but rarely both. This points to a paradox that Tocqueville explored in *Democracy in America*: A society that was highly *individualistic* was necessarily *collectivistic* at the same time.[5] He anticipated the concept of the mass society, a society in which the institutions of family and community have been weakened so that there is no buffer between the individual and public opinion and government. In a state of psychological weakness, unable to depend on family and friends for help, the individual turns to public opinion and government for direction in attitudes and behavior. As we have seen, Tocqueville understood public opinion as a civic or political religion. With his description of individualism in a democracy, he anticipated the emergence of personal religions that were "medicine" for the anxious individual.

Early on, Raymond Aron popularized the term "secular religion."[6] A secular religion is a "particular kind of ideology." It purports to be superior to and to supplant traditional monotheistic religions in the West. Secular religion may even cross national

5. Tocqueville, *Democracy in America*.

6. Aron, *Progress and Disillusion*.

boundaries in aspiring to be universal. Aron discussed Fascism, National Socialism, and Marxism-Leninism as examples. History soon revealed, however, that secular or political religion was efficacious only within national boundaries.

In *Redeemer Nation*, Ernest Tuveson examined American nationalism as a secular or political religion.[7] His study revealed that whereas the Puritans believed that they were destined to establish the "New Jerusalem," what we now call America was only its locus. By the nineteenth century, however, America itself was perceived to be a chosen people with a millennial mission to accomplish worldwide redemption. The "Manifest Destiny" of this exceptional people was to bring Christian principles married to American democracy and capitalism to the rest of the world. This was a utopian quest with a long life, for during the Vietnamese War, Lyndon Johnson would say that bringing American democracy (and American capitalism, of course) to the Vietnamese was a purpose of the war.

Robert Bellah used Rousseau's term "civil religion" to discuss what he thought every country possessed.[8] Eschewing Herberg's view that the American Way of Life was an expression of idolatry, Bellah argued that at its core civil religion was an ethical code that bound people together, and as such was not incompatible with Christianity and Judaism. Part of this ethical code is enshrined in the American Constitution. In his view religion can be more or less reduced to an ethical code.

In *Idols of the Tribe*, Harold Isaacs moves the discussion of secular, civil, or political religion from the nation to the ethnic group, race, linguistic group, and virtually every form of group identity.[9] This represents a "retribalization," the result of the American melting pot broken into group shards. Isaacs recognizes that historically religion and politics are inexorably linked so that a true separation of church and state is rare and ephemeral. Political group identity has strong religious overtones in retribalization.

7. Tuveson, *Redeemer Nation*.
8. Bellah, "Civil Religion."
9. Isaacs, *Idols of the Tribe*.

In *The Invisible Religion*, Thomas Luckmann analyzed the myriad of personal religions that we now encounter, arguing that the sacred cosmos, a part of a worldview, has become anomic so that a variety of "ultimate meanings" are located in the private sphere of life.[10] Personal identity is more important than group identity. Individual religiosity is a consumer choice unrelated to the primary institutions of religion and politics. The dominant theme of invisible religion is self-realization. Hence, it is possible for any consumer good or service to provide self-realization as advertising so emphatically tells us. Self-realization is ultimate meaning although self-realization is both fragile and transitory.

No one has provided a more detailed critique of personal or invisible religion than Donald Meyer.[11] In his 1965 *The Positive Thinkers*, Meyer demonstrated that the psychological individualism of the nineteenth century gave birth to "mind cure," a type of positive thinking, designed to return to health anxious Americans. Psychologically weak individuals were thrown into the competition of life under capitalism. All human relationships, not just economic relationships, had become competitive and uncertain. Mind cure was a way of bringing the individual back to mental health without disturbing the larger social order. Beginning as a secular enterprise, mind cure or positive thinking was quickly adopted by religious practitioners such as Norman Vincent Peale and Fulton J. Sheen. Even as a secular practice by Dale Carnegie, for example, it was an invisible religion. Pop psychology was a religion and religion was pop psychology.

By 2006 positive thinking as pop psychology was taken over by modern medicine. In *Artificial Happiness*, medical doctor Ronald Dworkin examined how the medical profession defined unhappiness as a disease. Working in tandem, psychiatrists and psychologists, on the one hand, and clergy, on the other hand, had attempted to counsel church members back to mental health, now termed happiness. Evidence indicated that mind cure or "soul

10. Luckmann, *The Invisible Religion*.
11. Meyer, *The Positive Thinkers*.

cure" was not working. Primary care physicians increasingly took over curing unhappiness with antidepressants.[12]

Concomitantly competitors entered the marketplace of happiness in the forms of alternative medicine, exercise, and spirituality. Spirituality is the most notable of these invisible religions because it has become independent of religion. Spirituality became an end in itself whose sole purpose was to create a sense of well-being. Modern medicine saw an opening, and doctors were free to recommend it along with antidepressants. People who practiced meditation or spirituality, we were told, lived longer, were healthier, and, most important, happier. Dworkin concluded, not without serious misgivings, that religion had lost out to medicine.

Martin Marty understood that Herberg's social map of religion provided in *Protestant, Catholic, Jew* applied to the time shortly after World War II. His 1976 book *A Nation of Behavers* includes in his new map the category of ethnic religion, not just civic religion, and a miscellaneous category, "new religions," which included a number of Eastern religious techniques, such as meditation, New Age religion, astrology, and even some religious cults. He divided Protestant Christianity into fundamentalist, evangelical, and mainline groups. He included of course Catholicism and Judaism. Marty's most important insight, in my view, was that the American Way of Life, under attack by the left in the 1960s, had found a home in evangelical churches. The book lacks, however, a theory that makes sense of this religious diversity.[13]

The aforementioned works were all struggling to understand major changes in traditional religions in the West and the rise of organized beliefs and practices that, while not calling themselves religious, functioned as such. The variety of names, secular religion, civil religion, civic religion, personal religion, invisible religion, pop psychology, and the like, were part of this search for understanding, with each author not completely happy with what his predecessor had done.

12. Dworkin, *Artificial Happiness*.
13. Marty, *Nation of Behavers*.

Herberg had come close to understanding the relationship between personal and public religion in showing how American democratic capitalism provided the opportunity and means to achieve peace of mind. This suggests that personal religion is a consumer service that capitalism makes possible. Religion as a consumer service is at the same time a psychological *technique*. This opens up another line of inquiry, one that Jacques Ellul has masterfully provided in *The New Demons*. In this book and others on technology, Ellul has analyzed how technology, which includes both material and nonmaterial (psychological and administrative techniques) technology, has become the chief determining factor in modern society at the same time it is collectively perceived to be sacred.[14]

## The Sacred

There is no more important and problematic concept in the cultural sciences than the sacred. The sacred encompasses more than organized religion; indeed, the latter is only one form a collective sense of the sacred can assume. The sacred has the following characteristics: (1) it is perceived to be of unlimited power; (2) it is regarded as that which is most real, the origin of reality; (3) it is considered to be of absolute value; (4) it is ambiguous in value; (5) it produces an ambivalent reaction on our part; (6) myths and rituals express the sacred: myth is the theory of the sacred, ritual its practice; (7) it is historical.

The sacred, Mircea Eliade maintains, is a spontaneous, collective creation.[15] We respond to the experience of unlimited power with our entire being. Not being a rational construction, the sacred is an intuition shared by the group. The concept of the sacred is a later development; first comes the experience.

The sacred is the origin of reality and as such our own existence. By living within the order, rituals, taboos, morality, law,

14. Ellul, *New Demons*.

15. Eliade, *Sacred and the Profane*; Eliade, *Patterns in Comparative Religion*.

and so forth, humans are alive to the purpose and significance of reality. The world becomes full of meaning and thus intelligible. The sacred is most real because it has the power to enhance life or bring death. We must attempt to control this power, to make it work for us.

The sacred is of absolute value and meaning flows from it. It is the anchor of culture. The profane is of lesser value; one of its meanings is the neutral. The division between sacred and profane allows us to create a hierarchy of values.

As power, the sacred includes negative and positive forces. It includes both that which we fear and that which we desire. Humans cannot fully control the negative aspects of life, nor can they always achieve what they desire. Born out of observation (from death comes new life) and out of desire, humans believe that the negative forces of life help bring about or renew the positive forces. The negative and positive forces are part of a larger totality, the environment in which we live.

Before examining how the sacred has changed over time, we need to look at Ellul's theory of the three milieus, a *descriptive* theory of history. In my view, it is the best theory of history we have, a theory that posits no underlying principle or logic to history, but remains close to the historical evidence.[16] A milieu is an environment, at once both material and symbolic, in which humans face their most formidable problems and from which they derive the means of survival and the meaning of life. A milieu has three basic characteristics: immediacy, sustenance and peril, and mediation. We are in immediate and direct relationship with our milieu; it forces us to adapt to it, just as surely we attempt to manipulate it. From the milieu we derive all that we need to live—sustenance for the body and spirit: food, clothing, shelter, order, and meaning. Concurrently, however, the milieu is the greatest threat to our existence, as in pestilence, famine, poisons, wild animals, political strife, wars, global warming, and widespread pollution. The milieu, then, is *ambiguous* in value and produces an *ambivalent* reaction—attraction and revulsion, desire and fear.

16. Ellul, *What I Believe*, 89–140.

A milieu is comprised of two divergent ingredients: meaning and power. Insofar as it is symbolic, a milieu is a human creation. The power of the milieu is harnessed for human ends; still, as an objective power, it is not fully under human control. A milieu assumes one of three forms: nature, society, or technology. The milieu is geographically and historically specific. For example, if you live near mountains or the ocean, this is nature for you; if you live in a desert, this is your nature.

Each subsequent milieu, society in relation to nature, technology in relation to society, mediates our relationship to the preceding one, rendering it an indirect force. The preceding milieu becomes an ideological model for the subsequent, thereby providing a justification for the new order, e.g., the concept of natural law in the milieu of society. In dialectical fashion, however, it is actually the subsequent milieu that is used to interpret the preceding one. For example, in the milieu of society, nature is read through society: it is anthropomorphized. Human society is projected onto nature as with divinities, social hierarchy, law, and a myriad of human passions that the gods express in myth. Therefore, nature as a model for society is to great extent a nature that is already a reflection of society.

Similarly, society serves as an ideological model in the milieu of technology. Computers have intelligence, memories, and languages. But it is a society controlled by technical rules and a technical logic and thereby rendered technological. Each preceding milieu continues to exert an influence on the subsequent one, but its threat appears less important most of the time. In the milieu of nature, the major problems are wild animals, poisons, and natural disasters; in the milieu of society the greatest threats are moral, political, and military conflicts; in the milieu of technology, threats include global warming, widespread pollution, and the destruction of language and culture. Not only does the subsequent milieu mediate the previous one, but it exacerbates the tensions and conflicts of the preceding one. For example, technology aggravates political and economic problems in the milieu of society, as witnessed by increasing ethnic, racial, and nationalistic strife about the economic benefits of technology.

Humans began the slow transition from the milieu of nature to the milieu of society perhaps nine to eleven thousand years ago, depending on geographical location and population density. The milieu of society arose with the emergence of towns and the emergence of civilizations at least six thousand years ago. The movement to the milieu of technology occurred in the nineteenth century and became fully established with the widespread use of the computer in the twentieth century. Ellul's theory is no finalist theory in which the last stage represents the end of history. Moreover, there is no determining principle underlying the process, no necessary movement to the next stage. Various societies can be in different stages in any period of history. Furthermore, there is no sense of progress: each milieu involves both gain and loss.

The sacred is in the most general sense the milieu. What better fits Eliade's definition of the sacred as power and reality than the milieu? That the milieu places us in an unresolvable situation of nurture and danger is the source of the ambiguity of sacred value. Roger Caillois's theory of the sacred explains the basic ambiguity: The sacred is both that which is holy and pure and that which is evil and defiling; likewise the profane is that which is evil and defiling and that which is neutral.[17] His deft linguistic analysis reveals that rather than two terms—sacred and profane—there are actually three terms—"sacred of respect," "sacred of transgression," and "profane" (as neutral). The term "sacred of *transgression*" is implicit in the natural languages he examined; it existed without conceptualization. The idea of sacred of transgression is derived from the meaning common to both terms "sacred" and "profane"—defilement. The fundamental tension a milieu presents us with is responsible for our ambivalence toward the power of the sacred.

Both Caillois and Eliade understood the ambiguity of the sacred as a consequence of creation emerging from chaos (natural or moral evil) and requiring periodic renewal. Moreover, they

17. Caillois, *Man and the Sacred.*

understood that nature and society consist of opposing forces so linked together that the renewal of the milieu involved the movement from one pole (chaos, death, evil) to the opposite pole (creation, life, good). The perceived need for renewal reveals the experience of a milieu as dynamic and not static. The milieu only exists by renewing itself. The festival is the ritualized movement from chaos to creation.

In the prehistoric period, nature is experienced as sacred, manifested in specific hierophanies (a spiritual power) embedded in the physical world, such as a sacred mountain. The two cosmic poles that organize the milieu of nature are life and death. The principle of regeneration is the feast, a ritualized meal. Food (especially meat when available) and eating symbolize the movement from death to life and permit communion with what is eaten. The festival, which is the ritualization of the experience of regeneration, is, in this instance, the feast.

In the historic period, both nature and society are experienced as sacred, but nature has the face of society. Deities in the milieu of society face the same moral and political tensions and conflicts that humans do. Sacred history, partially freed from the circular time of nature, is the history of the ancestors and becomes more important than the cosmogony. Eventually the earthly king becomes sacred and may even be seen to be the ruler of nature. The aristocratic class comes to be perceived as quasi-sacred, as the important descendants of the ancestors. Church and state are intertwined even with a necessary division of labor so that both organize the milieu of society.

Religion, morality, and politics arise in the milieu of society as the most pressing problems become human relationships. Religion organizes the experience of the sacred in a more rational way than the symbolism of myth and ritual alone could. The entire movement of the milieu of society is toward greater rationality and individuality. Religion creates a liturgy, a code of ethics, a theology, and church organization. This rational superstructure rests upon the infrastructure of myth and ritual that spontaneously and symbolically express the experience of the sacred.

Politics too surfaces in the milieu of society and with greater differentiation within the division of labor partially separates itself from the institution of religion. As two types of authority, one ostensibly sacred, the other less obviously so, they are mutually accommodating. Political society is always ready to supplant religious society as the dominant force. The history of comparative religion indicates that a true separation of church and state is rare and transitory.

In the milieu of society, the polar tension is between good and evil. Strictly speaking, sacred and profane as moral terms only arise in this milieu. Eliade observed that before the undesired parts of life were considered as punishment for moral transgressions, they were regarded as constituent parts of nature—as "natural evil."[18] The idea of retribution becomes a universal principle encompassing nature and society. Good deeds are rewarded, evil deeds are punished. This is the origin of the theory of causality.[19] Natural disasters are perceived as punishment for moral transgression. Sacrifice, of which scapegoating is central in the milieu of society, represents the expulsion of evil. The scapegoat is responsible for evil and its punishment. By removing the scapegoat from society, order (the good) can be restored.[20] Sacrifice, Caillois argued, is the inner mechanism of the festival.

The festival is enlarged to include, in addition to the feast, sacrifice of the scapegoat and the ritual performance of tabooed actions (a return to chaos). To the chaos of suffering and death is added moral chaos. Taboo and its violation are artifacts of the milieu of society.

In the post-historic period, where time is linear and quantitative, as in the myth of progress, both society and technology are experienced as sacred, but now society is read through technology. Moral and political problems are transformed into technical problems left to be solved by experts. For many in Silicon Valley, an algorithm for every decision and problem is on the horizon. Evgeny

18. Eliade, *Patterns in Comparative Religion*.

19. Kelsen, *Society and Nature*.

20. Girard, *Scapegoat*; Stivers, "Festival in Light."

Morozov calls this "technological solutionism."[21] Technology is both power and reality today. Although at one level technology is abstract as rational and logical information, at another level it is material as a world of technical objects. The attempt to quantify all attitudes and actions in an algorithm is to turn attitudes and actions into material objects. This is the way technology creates the homogeneity necessary for its continued growth.

A technological society is one whose chief value, purpose, and goal is rational *efficiency*. Over against rational technique stands inefficiency as instinct, eros, the will to power. The technological milieu transforms good and evil into solutions (good) to problems (evil) that technology can provide. For every technical problem there is a technical solution. Every problem is a matter of inefficiency, and every solution makes for greater efficiency. The opposite poles, efficiency and inefficiency, are at a deeper level related. As Ellul notes, technology and instinctual power form a dialectic: Today desire can only be satisfied by technology, and technology can only advance by the constant stimulation of appetite. Jean Brun first called attention to the paradox that the cold, impersonal, abstract force of technology does not finally appeal to reason and moderation but to our insatiable desire for power and consumption.[22]

The more reason becomes objectified and thus collectivized in the technological system, the smaller the role for subjective reason based on experience. This tends to enlarge the play of irrational or instinctual forces; moreover, the cumulative impact of technology represses us. The more technology demands of us in regulations, schedules, and coordination, the more we need to escape technical rationality by plunging into irrationality, random sensations, and ecstatic experiences.[23] The result is a society both extraordinarily rational and irrational.[24]

21. Morozov, *To Save Everything*.

22. Cited in Ellul, *New Demons*.

23. Ellul, *Technological Society*, 387–427.

24. Stivers, *Technology as Magic*.

The instincts most associated with the will to power are sexuality and aggression. Indeed, sex and violence act as the sacred of transgression over against the technological order. As instinctual power, they represent inefficiency and are the negative pole to the positive pole of efficiency as technology. If a milieu is composed of two poles in tension, and the principle of regeneration involves the movement from the negative power to the positive power, then in this milieu that principle is excessive, experimental consumption.[25] Technology, while manifestly opposed to instinct, is similar to it at a deeper level because both represent the will to power. Illustrative is advertising's use of sex and violence to sell consumer goods, as with the long-standing eroticizing of the automobile and motorcycle. Even more important than advertising's direct use of sex and violence is its indirect use of them: The consumer goods (technical objects) of advertising are placed in spatial relation to the sex-and-violence–saturated programs of the media. In this sense such programs are ads for advertisements. The consumption of the instinctual power of sex and violence increases the desire to consume technical objects, services, and information. The motto is: the more we consume sexual and violent images, the more technical objects, services, and information we will consume; the more objects, services, and information we consume, the more instinctual power we possess.

Caillois observes that excess is at the "heart of the festival."[26] The more one pushes the negative pole, the greater the abundance at the positive pole. In the milieu of technology, the festival is centered in the excess of sexual and violent images in the media. As the ritualization of the principle of regeneration, the festival begins with chaos, the negative pole—death, evil, inefficiency (instinct)—in the movement to creation, the positive pole—life, good, efficiency (technical rationality).

In the milieu of technology, society is still sacred but in a secondary way. Society has been transformed by technology. Society becomes the nation-state in the milieu of technology. Largely

25. Stivers, *Technology as Magic.*
26. Caillois, *Man and the Sacred.*

through technology in the form of bureaucracy, military power, and propaganda, political power in the state became formidable. Nationalism was a necessary adjunct to the growing power of state—we had to identify with the state so that it became our state. The sacred poles of transformed society became the nation-state and revolution. Ellul's discussion of the sacred axis of political power is insightful.[27] The political state operates solely by force as it has continued to grow over the past five centuries.[28] Political revolutions, including terrorism, are necessarily violent in their quest to gain the power of the state. Revolutionary violence matches and must surpass the violence of the political state.

Political revolution leads to a renewal of the political state. Whether successful or not, political revolutions force the state to grow stronger. Political revolutions over the past two centuries have only led to an increase in the power of the state.[29] The real question is not which political class or revolutionary group has power, but the power of the state itself. Today the nation is comprised of a plethora of special interest groups, all relentlessly competing for access to and control of the political state. But power has become abstract and resides in the technological system whose chief client is the political state.

Desacralization occurs in the sacred of transgression in relation to the sacred of respect. It is a necessary part of renewal. But desacralization, as Ellul observed, occurs when a new sacred supplants the established one.[30] Christianity succeeded in desacralizing the sacred deities of the Roman Empire, but then the church eventually became sacred. Money and then technology desacralized the church and then themselves became sacred. The sacred is historically relative and promiscuous in regard to power.

---

27. Ellul, *New Demons.*
28. Jouvenel, *On Power.*
29. Ellul, *Autopsy of Revolution.*
30. Ellul, *New Demons.*

## Personal Religion

Secular religion includes both personal and political religion. In a technological society both are essential. Personal religion is religion that can be customized to my needs and preferences. It is born out of the interiorization of human reality. J. H. van den Berg, a historical psychologist, has described this transformation. Until the late eighteenth century in the West, the individual's consciousness was largely one with the other members of the community. Certainly each individual was different, but all members of the community shared a common morality that bound a status group, e.g., men, to other status groups, e.g., women, resulting in an organic community with moral ties among both individuals and groups. Consequently, consciousness was first collective before it was singular.[31]

With the decline of a common morality, relationships between groups and between individuals became vague and uncertain. Individualism emerged and began to take root. Without the trust that moral expectations had provided, a certain loneliness set in, along with a mild fear of others. What remained common was a minimal understanding of the social world—facts about empirical reality. All understanding of meaning, aesthetical, ethical, and religious qualities, retreated into an inner self (no longer one with the community). All discourse about meaning, every aspect of culture, every institution became multivalent. With a wealth of possible meanings each individual had to create her own understanding.

Van den Berg maintains that the discipline of psychology arose to deal with the new inner self. The multivalent social world presented the individual with the problems of making the correct choice—marriage, career, belief. All the human sciences were drafted into service to help the individual adjust to an uncertain world and uncertain future and to conform to a social world of ephemeral norms. Anxiety was a necessary condition of the autonomous inner self.

---

31. Van den Berg, *Changing Nature of Man*.

Anxiety is accompanied by alienation. Ellul maintains that the alienation today is more abstract than the political and economic alienation of the recent past.[32] Each technique attacks the individual. Each technique is specialized and has as its object only a part of the individual, whether mental, emotional, or physical. Advertising, for example, reifies each need and each desire in order to manipulate the consumer. The multitude of human techniques fragment the individual.[33] The solution to the uncertainty and anxiety that accompanies fragmentation is psychological technique. Problem and solution are one. We saw earlier that the more rigid and demanding the technological system is, the greater the need for ecstatic escape. This need is also met by psychological technique, including those we have called "personal religion."

Personal religion is related to the sacred axis with technology as the sacred of respect and sex and violence in the media as the sacred of transgression. The main appeal of technology to the individual is the promise of increased consumption. The consumption of technical objects, services, and information is compensation for the individual's servitude to the technological system and its repressive impact upon him.

In *The Technological Society*, Ellul observed that technology unites magical and mystical techniques, which historically were opposed. Eliade demonstrated that magic, which was a way of controlling the external environment, was radically different from mysticism, which was a technique for controlling one's inner life.[34] He asserted that cultures and even civilizations could be identified as more magically or mystically inclined. Psychological technique applied to others' functions as a kind of magic, when applied to self as a form of mysticism.[35]

Mysticism is spiritual self-transformation. It represents an individual attempt to unite oneself with nature, a god, or the

32. Ellul, *Technological Society*.

33. Fragmentation results in individuals who are role players confused about their identity. See Van den Berg, *Changing Nature of Man*.

34. Eliade, *Patterns in Comparative Religion*.

35. Stivers, *Technology as Magic*.

universe. It involves an escape from the conscious self to achieve an altered state of consciousness. Most often mysticism was associated with a religious philosophy.

Mysticism allows one to achieve a state of ecstasy. Another type of ecstasy can be achieved in a communal setting through loud, repetitive music, chanting and dancing, frenzied activity, drugs, alcohol, and violence, all of which lead to an ecstatic state, an altered state of consciousness. Victor Turner has described the ecstasy acquired in a communal setting as "communitas," a feeling of communion with every other participant, who has for the moment become one's equal. A feeling of one in all and all in one.[36] Cultural anthropologists have a category, ecstatic religion, to describe any religion whose primary purpose is ecstasy.

If a technological society fosters the need for an ecstatic escape from a society too tightly organized, the escape into mysticism and group ecstasy can meet as well the need to escape the fear, anxiety, alienation, and loneliness it creates. Psychological technique becomes the "solution" that technology manufactures in the first place. Psychological technique, however, furthers alienation in subjecting the individual to still more technology.

Mysticism and communal ecstasy involve communion with something beyond oneself to the point of identity: I become what I behold. Communion with nature, a god, other people, but now with a machine, yet invariably an escape from one's conscious self.

The technology/sex-violence sacred axis centers around consumption for the individual. Virtually every kind of technical object, service, and information can become an ephemeral personal religion. Vegetarianism, environmentalism, gun ownership, membership in a Corvette club, pornography, sports, New Age, astrology, and alternative medicine are among the myriad of choices. Spirituality is an apt example today.

Ronald Dworkin, a doctor, traces the gradual separation of spirituality from religion and the reduction of spirituality to an autonomous feeling about which doctors could have a say. Neuroscience, Dworkin suggests, implied that spirituality was "religion's

36. Turner, *Ritual Process.*

active beneficial ingredient" and that spirituality was a feeling located in the central nervous system. Doctors wanted in on the game, and became supporters of spirituality, touting its benefit to one's overall health and sense of well-being. It didn't matter what one was spiritual about as long as one practiced spirituality. A legion of spiritual techniques and self-help books appeared overnight.[37]

Spirituality is the stepchild of the positive thinking movement that began in the nineteenth century.[38] Positive thinking or mind cure was based on the idea that the solution to one's problems in life involved thinking the correct thought, a kind of self-hypnosis. Health, happiness, and success were promised. The main difference between positive thinking and spirituality was that the former was to be achieved by thought, whereas the latter was to be obtained by leaving conscious thought behind for an altered state of consciousness, a mystical state. Consequently, positive thinking was a kind of magic one performed on oneself, but the result was the same. Positive thinking or mind cure involved repetition of thought and words, even chanting, which when performed for a long enough period produced an ecstatic state. It was a kind of mysticism after all. Herberg addressed this later in the 1950s when he referred to personal religion as an anodyne in the attempt to achieve peace of mind.[39] Peace of mind was a feeling, a state of mild ecstasy. He maintained that this was now the principal form religion assumed.

Side by side with the mystical forms of personal religion stand the techniques to achieve ecstasy by speed, repetition, or crowd frenzy. Included are sports, esports, video games, gambling, and social media. Sports as a religion is well understood, whether one thinks of soccer "madness" or the frenzy of American football fans. The word "fan" comes from the word "fanatic." The most religious or addictive psychological techniques are gambling, video

---

37. Dworkin, *Artificial Happiness*.

38. Meyer, *Positive Thinkers*.

39. Herberg, *Protestant, Catholic, Jew*.

RELIGION IN AMERICA TODAY

games, and social media. These technologies all involve in one way or the other communion with the machine.

Technological repression creates a need for escape, as we have seen. Milan Kundera observed that "speed is the form of ecstasy the technological revolution has bestowed on man."[40] We internalize technological stimuli and adjust to and normalize the ways technology alters our sense of time, place, speed, sight, and sound.[41] We demand faster and faster computers and smartphones as we internalize the speed of slower ones and desire to live ever more quickly. We thus come to resemble the ever faster technology that makes us respond reflexively not reflectively.[42]

If technology creates a need for ecstatic release, it also produces the means to achieve it. Machine gambling is a prime example. In *Addiction by Design*, Natasha Schüll interviews gambling adults in Las Vegas and discovers that more than winning they crave to be in the "zone," in which "time, space, and social identity are suspended in the mechanical rhythm of a repeating process"— in other words, a state of ecstasy. Gamblers enter the zone when their actions and the functioning of the machine become indistinguishable. Schüll uses the term "perfect contingency" to describe the feeling that gamblers, especially the addicted, have of a perfect alignment between their actions and the machine's response. They prefer "sameness, repetition, rhythm, and routine." Slot machines and video poker are the most popular gambling formats. As gamblers become acclimated to the speed of the machine, they desire faster and more complex games. For instance, in video poker, Triple Play Draw Poker allows players to play three games at once and make three times as many bets. Triple Play has given way to Five Play, Ten Play, Fifty Play, and even Hundred Play poker.[43] Schüll interviewed gamblers whose addiction fit the clinical definition. She recognized that there were "addicts" whose compulsion fell short of this definition. Without getting into a long discussion of

40. Kundera, *Slowness*, 2.
41. Stivers, *Shades of Loneliness*.
42. Stivers, *Shades of Loneliness*.
43. Schüll, *Addiction by Design*.

whether or not there are degrees of addiction, I am using the term in its colloquial sense: something we can't seem to stop doing even though it's not necessary for our survival.

Video game enthusiasts too desire to merge with the machine, thereby entering into communion with it. The player, the characters in the game, and the technology itself become one. In *God in the Machine: Video Games as Spiritual Pursuit*, Liel Leibovitz, a video game player himself, describes how reflex replaces cognitive awareness the greater one's skill and mastery becomes.[44] His experience is largely with The Legend of Zelda. Repetition is the foundation of play, from the "ballet of thumbs" to the return to the same play section without stop and with little if any variation. The spiritual pursuit that Leibovitz claims is the deeper rationale for playing video games as ecstasy. If ecstatic religion is a legitimate category of religion, then video games are a subcategory. In defense of his interpretation, Leibovitz argues that video games teach one the joy of learning to love the game and its designer above all (veiled reference to life and God), of giving up "all other ways of being in the world" and of "understanding one's place in the world." Clearly this ecstatic religion has ascetic overtones. He calls this an Augustinian condition.

Social media are not ostensibly about communion with a machine but with other people. Every technology that allows us to communicate with others mediates the relationship, however. The stronger the mediation, the more abstract and impersonal the relationship becomes. The mediating technology imposes conditions and rules of use. It is questionable, then, with whom you are primarily communicating. Social media "addicts" appear to spend less time servicing their addiction than do gambling and video game devotees. Still, a larger number of social media users admit they cannot relinquish their devices, if only for a day. Some are even bedeviled by phantom ringing or vibrating phones, checking their phones hundreds of times a day. The ostensible purpose of social media is to allow us to sustain our community of family and friends.

44. Leibovitz, *God in the Machine.*

In *Alone Together*, Sherry Turkle discovered that the community of one's friends, say on Facebook, is both fragile and enslaving.[45] On social media platforms, people tend to become role players, presenting a self to others that will be most accepted and admired. The new relationships established through social media platforms are superficial. Indeed, the more time one spends on Facebook, the more lonely one feels. Turkle observes that many young people prefer texting to talking: A call involves more commitment than a text. A call could prove demanding and unpleasant.

At the same time, however, social media produce "group feelings," an ecstatic "communion with others." The very speed of communication momentarily intensifies group feelings, even if they remain superficial. Elias Canetti refers to a group that becomes a unified whole an "open crowd," the truest expression of the crowd phenomenon. Within the open crowd there exists a sense of absolute equality (communitas), because all divisions among people are momentarily obliterated in the common support of a cause or common rejection of an enemy. The ecstasy of communitas is a necessary component of the open crowd.[46] The ecstasy that ensues from the use of a social media platform is not communion that creates true community, but the anxious communication within an open crowd, always poised to become a mob. Social media platforms work to create ecstasy in the speed with which members of the open crowd communicate with one another. When one retreats from the crowd, however, loneliness and anxiety return.

The technology that best illustrates the opposite poles of the sacred axis is the video game. The act of renewal is the movement from the negative pole to the positive pole. From sexual and violent images to images of victory. Video games are saturated with eroticized violence, but the point of the game is to win. Sex and violence are the power of instinct, technology the power of rationality. The video game is all about images of sacred power. The victor exercises a superior use of technology or its equivalent,

45. Turkle, *Alone Together*.
46. Canetti, *Crowds and Power*.

magic. The loser suffers the ultimate defeat—a violent death. The implication is that the greater the violence the more efficient technology must become. The festival of the video game is represented in the ecstatic state of the players. The festival is about excess, as Caillois noted, and if it is about anything, the video game is about excess—speed, information, images. Certainly the negative pole of the sacred axis is present in the use of pornography on the Internet and in contact sports, a type of ritualized violence. But the video game best captures the spirit of the festival.

Now some may object that it is far fetched to call this religion, even personal religion. Keep in mind that ecstatic rituals to create communitas are not marginal and unimportant but an essential part of the ritual process in traditional societies.

The need for ecstasy that a technological society stimulates is not satisfied by an occasional ritual performance. It is an ongoing response to the ever-greater controls exercised over us. The repression of a technological society is unrelenting. Consequently, our need for ecstasy becomes addictive. We are increasingly aware of our various addictions to technology and use the word "addiction" more frequently, but we neither understand their causes nor recognize their identity as personal religions.

Personal religion includes both mystical self-transformation and ritualized ecstasy. It can be a psychological technique or an addiction to a material technology or object. Personal religion at best provides ephemeral and superficial satisfaction, reducing the meaning of life to its lowest level. This is why it is possible to have multiple personal religions simultaneously. Personal religions make no exclusive demand on us, for they exist solely as consumer choices.

Personal religion cannot unite a society, crafted as it is to meet individual needs and desires. A technological milieu turns everything into an imitation of technology or a compensation for its impact.[47] Technology is empirical and reduces every quality to quantity so as to be measured. This makes for what Vahanian calls radical immanentism, a belief that our world is a self-contained

---

47. Ellul, *Perspectives on Our Age.*

material reality.[48] Religion, as we will see, cannot serve to unite a fully materialistic world without meaning, but only offer it comfort. Politics now fills the void that religion once filled.

Martin Marty and R. Scott Appleby's study of worldwide fundamentalist religious groups in the 1980s revealed that most important to these groups was their political and social agenda even though they had a religious identity.[49] They had a desire to remake a world perceived to be in chaos by politically imposing their rigid moral code on it. Each fundamentalist group had an authoritarian leader. It appears they were political groups with a religious veneer. Overtly authoritarian political leaders abound today so that fundamentalist religious movements and authoritarian political movements appear to have become one movement.

48. Vahanian, *Death of God.*

49. Marty and Appleby, *Glory and the Power.* The authors borrowed the term "fundamentalist religion" from certain conservative Protestant groups and applied this to similar groups all over the world. Consequently, there are fundamentalist Islamic groups, Hindu groups, Jewish groups, and even Buddhist groups, among others.

CHAPTER 4

# Political Religion

*No politics ever has, no politics ever can, no worldliness ever has, no worldliness ever can, think through or realize to its last consequences the thought of human equality. To realize complete equality in the medium of worldliness, i.e. to realize it in the medium the very nature of which implies differences, and to realize it in a worldly way, i.e. by positing differences—such a thing is forever impossible, as is apparent from the categories. For if complete equality were to be attained, worldliness would be at an end.*

—SØREN KIERKEGAARD
*THE POINT OF VIEW FOR MY WORK AS AN AUTHOR*

## From Religion to Politics

THE NATION-STATE/REVOLUTION SACRED AXIS gives rise to political religion. Ellul is not just talking about political religion being one form of religion among many religions, as with the usual discussion of civic or civil religion. He asserts that only political religion can unite a group today. Religion as we have previously known it cannot provide the symbolic meaning that unites a society, for it has been reduced to the status of personal religion, in other words, an individual consumer choice. How did we get to this point? Ellul's theory of the three milieus provides one answer. Two theories, one by Owen Barfield, the other by Gilbert Simondon, also help us understand this momentous change. Both are consistent with the theory of the three milieus.

Barfield's *Saving the Appearances: A Study in Idolatry* identifies three historical forms of symbolization and conceptualization that help to explain how the institution of religion lost its ability to provide symbolic meaning for society.[1] The farther back we go, Barfield argues, the more thinking was symbolic.[2] Symbolization depends on the tacit perception that the world is an organic totality. Unlike concepts, which differentiate phenomena as autonomous entities, symbols express a sense of unity by perceiving relations of similarity between apparently divergent phenomena, e.g., tree and water and life; heart and courage, sincerity, and love: tree and water symbolize life; heart symbolizes courage, sincerity, and love. The former example tree and water illustrates the tendency of various symbols to share a meaning; the latter example demonstrates the need of a symbol to move extensively within the organic unity of nature or society to make multiple connections among the parts by way of comparison. In either instance a symbol can not be reduced to a discrete meaning or refer to a single entity. The result is a symbolic organic unity. Symbolization involves the attribution of "inwardness" or "consciousness" to a world believed to be fully alive. Meaning in the strong sense of the term is inwardness or that which is qualitative in the form of feelings, states of mind, moral qualities, and the like. By contrast, a logical concept attempts to capture all possible meanings at a high level of abstraction. The higher the level of abstraction, however, the less meaning is conveyed. Just consult a dictionary for a definition of love. The farther back we go in the milieu of nature, the more these qualities were believed to be dimensions of *action*, rather than "immaterial

1. Barfield, *Saving the Appearances*.

2. A symbol provides indirect meaning through comparison. In contrast a logical concept offers us a direct, abstract meaning. The more we employ logical concepts the more abstract is our view of reality.

beings," like Platonic ideals. For example, love is a quality of how one person *treats* another person rather than an idea that we express in words. Prior to the emphasis on human action, we saw love as a quality of how nature acts on and with us. Human love was part of the love that existed in a vibrant nature.

The name for such action is "participation." Humans felt part of that organic totality called the world, whose power is first spiritual. Participation entails a tacit recognition that humans are part of a world whose consciousness is embedded in human consciousness. Language is a creative force born out of the interaction between the spirit or consciousness of nature and human spirit. This emotional and spiritual link between nature and humans allows us to name and attribute qualities, collective representations, to the world and thus participate in its ongoing creation. Humans are, as it were, allowing nature to work in and through them. Therefore, phenomena only fully come into existence when they are named. This form of participation, which occurs in the milieu of nature, is called "original participation" by Barfield.

Original participation in the symbolic creation of nature did not occur in a fully conscious way. In the transition to the milieu of society, however, humans began to think rationally about the world and their place in it. Throughout most of the historic period (milieu of society), rational thinking remains secondary to symbolic understanding of nature and human existence. Myth, story, and poetry created the meaning that philosophy attempted to define and later science denied. As long as humans retained a sense that perceived phenomena were created in part out of their own conceptions, that they participated in their collective representations of the world and human society, they avoided the positivism of believing that their concepts were a reflection of the way things were in themselves.

In the milieu of society, Barfield maintains, inwardness moves from nature to human society. Nature now becomes a part of human consciousness. Humans still possessed a sense of a spiritual power beyond themselves. Nature and society were perceived as organic totalities so similar they formed a larger unity. The ethical and aesthetical qualities of human culture now became the paramount symbols used to make sense of nature. Rational thought still rested on a bed of symbolic representations.

The next stage, the post-historic[3] (milieu of technology) involves the denial we participate in our symbolization and conceptualization. With positivism we come to believe that our concepts capture reality, that there is a one-to-one relationship between them. Barfield refers to this as idolatry, mistaking our concepts for reality and thereby creating idols of our own beliefs. Our reified concepts are like visual images of our own creation to which we attribute spiritual power.

The vast symbolic edifice of nature and society begins to disintegrate in the milieu of technology. If only an organic unity suggests symbolization, the reverse is true as well: only a symbolic environment appears to be organic. Traditional symbolism declined because this mode of understanding is incongruent with the milieu of technology. Logical thought, namely technical thought, is now triumphant. To understand reality in terms of cause and effect, it has first to be broken into ever smaller discrete parts, and then reassembled according to causal or probabilistic relations. The implication is that the technological milieu is not experienced as an organic whole.

Science and technology have become so pervasive and dominant that nature and human society are reduced to empirical or material reality. The technological milieu is dependent on the technological system, an abstract system of information that works to coordinate various technologies at the level of action.[4] Each individual technology thus becomes a means of acting and a source of information for other technologies. Each subsystem of the technological system, e.g., transportation, industry, and communication, has to be coordinated with other subsystems. This system of information is formed out of specialized bits of information and algorithms that are symbolically meaningless but

3. *Post-historic* means that the past as symbolic collective experience is replaced by the objectified abstract knowledge of technology.

4. Ellul, *Technological System*.

necessary for establishing causal relations between technologies. The technological system exhibits holism at the level of *causality* or probability, not *meaning*. Technical thought, Ellul observes, which is "simplifying, reductive, operational, instrumental, and rearranging," creates the system.

There is an inverse relationship between the power of technology and the human need to symbolize. Historically, symbolization was a way for humans to exercise some control over their milieu. By enveloping it within their symbol systems in narratives, even as they were acknowledging its greater power, they gained a sense of mastery. Ellul argues that the human ability to symbolize has been the single most important factor in the social evolution of the human race.[5] Because technology is our own creation we do not perceive the need to symbolize it in the traditional sense. It is only when we confront a foreign power such as nature that we bring it within our symbolic net. Symbolization both creates a meaningful world and allows us to distance ourselves from this world. Without effective symbolization we have no way to prevent technology from invading and conquering culture. Today symbolization occurs in the media but it is multivalent, hollow, and ephemeral. The symbolization is mainly through the visual image that only establishes a correlation between the image and its object without any meaning. The pseudo-symbols are used for purposes of manipulation in propaganda, advertising, and public relations. There is now no critical distance between technology and us. The visual images in the media are the way *technology symbolizes itself.* It refuses to allow the distance between technology and us necessary for us to gain control over our technological milieu.

Only a symbolic universe gives us the experience of living in a "concrete reality." When language becomes too abstract, reduced entirely to logical concepts, we are cut off from reality and inhabit a world of personified abstractions. When language loses meaning, we live solely in a material, empirical world of instinct, sensation, and power that the visual images of the media create.[6]

5. Ellul, "Symbolic Function."
6. Stivers, *Technology as Magic.*

And this is a frightening world of raw power, within which one must always be suspicious and distrustful of others; moreover, it is a world that always appears on the verge of apocalypse.[7] Only symbolic discourse allows us to create and experience a world of aesthetical and ethical meaning, a world that appears coherent, consistent, and worthy of trust. Concrete reality is a unified reality; only a symbolic universe can unite the abstract and the material. Without effective symbolism, humans live within a fragmented and dangerous world.

The implication of Barfield's theory is that with the decline of symbolic meaning, religion in its traditional sense becomes impossible. The institution of religion requires symbolization applicable to the present; technology does not.

Gilbert Simondon's theory is likewise congruent with Ellul's theory of the three milieus.[8] Simondon posits that in prehistory, the milieu of nature, humans had a completely magical view of the world and a magical way of acting on and with nature. Magic was both a worldview and a means of action. As technology developed, it was first applied to the physical environment. Consequently, magic as a worldview is fractured. At this point, religion developed to provide the worldview (system of symbols) that magic had previously done. In the milieu of technology, as technology is applied to the psychological and spiritual life of humans, it meets all human needs and thus makes the institution of religion irrelevant. There is no need or place for religion that symbolizes our existence. Technical logic supplants symbolic thought in making all reality solely material. The institution of religion lives on as traditional symbolism that does not apply to a technological society. It survives as nostalgia for the past and principally as a psychological technique in the present. Politics becomes the only way to provide a worldview in a radically material world. Politics can provide an ideology that applies to a group struggling to maintain or to acquire power. The political group may be national, racial, ethnic, or based on sexual identity. The ideology offers the group a better life

7. Ellul, *Humiliation of the Word.*
8. Simondon, *Existence of Technical Objects.*

in this world, our only world. If there is no transcendent meaning, no afterlife, then we must be concerned with the power to make life as comfortable and secure as possible now. The symbolism in political ideology is not symbolism that provides meaning but the pseudo-symbolism of the technological milieu. It is now a servant of propaganda. Propaganda, Ellul noted over fifty years ago, has become autonomous: it uses ideology to further the group's struggle to achieve or retain power. Propaganda is technical and like all technology answers only to effectiveness and efficiency.[9] Ellul makes use of Simondon's theory in *The New Demons*.[10] Political religion has been transformed into politics. To remain viable all traditional religions are reduced to personal religion or are forced to make their political and moral agenda a top priority, that is, turn politics into religion.

Politics is now aligned with technology, not religion and morality. With the politicization of every action and decision each problem becomes simultaneously a political and a technical problem. With the decline of a common morality and political idealism, politics is reduced to power, and the only unity a society can achieve is through creating an ultimate enemy, the scapegoat who threatens the group. With power the rationale for politics, and even with a scapegoat, political unity is fragile and ephemeral. Consequently, each racial, ethnic, gender, and special interest group becomes a miniature nation, desiring to make its interests one with the larger nation. Each political party wants to make government its fiefdom. Political discourse reveals that these groups now inhabit mutually exclusive worlds.

## Truth, Reality, Possibility: From Ideology to Conspiracy Theory

Discourse today is under suspicion. It seems to be made up of nothing but rumor, ideological statements, and conspiracy

9. Ellul, *Propaganda*.
10. Ellul, *New Demons*.

theories. Can we believe anything we hear today? Truth, reality, and facts suffer the consequences. Kierkegaard discussed the relationship between what is true and what is false.[11] They are not equal in meaning, but exist in a hierarchy. Truth defines both itself and its opposite, falsehood.

Truth is a difficult and elusive concept. In traditional religious cultures, truth was transcendent and as such was understood to be absolute and derived from the sacred.[12] To tell the truth meant that one's words were in accord with mythological beliefs and religious teachings. With the triumph of science and the reduction of a symbolic reality to a purely material reality, truth was reduced to fact. Truth was that which could be established as factual. But truth didn't stop with science. As Barfield understood over sixty years ago, truth had become technological.[13] A technological society only values ideas and facts insofar as they further the means of action. *Truth is powerful action.* When technology becomes truth—the ability to manipulate reality—then true and false become equal and the difference in value disappears. The result is a world of unconstrained power. True is what I say and do, false is what you (my enemy) say and do. Truth becomes whatever I want it to be.

Truth can be contrasted with empirical reality (that which is material and quantifiable) as well. In *The Humiliation of the Word*, Ellul demonstrates that discourse allows us to explore what truth is.[14] The visual image is best suited to allow us to traverse empirical reality. Vision enables us to see empirical reality and make use of it for our purposes. The visual images of the media change the balance, however. We are now flooded with visual images of our own creation, not merely images that nature provides us with. The

11. Kierkegaard, *Sickness Unto Death.*

12. For Christians, truth is the Word of God, Jesus Christ, his words and actions. Christ's actions perfectly correspond to his words and express love as the way of nonpower. By contrast, technology is ultimately violent as the most powerful means of action.

13. Barfield, *Saving the Appearances.*

14. Ellul, *Humiliation of the Word.*

technologically created visual image has become more important than discourse. The universe of visual images has become the "language" of technology, showing what it is and can be. With the triumph of the visual image, language has become its adjunct. Words are "explained" by images. If there is no truth, only empirical reality, then everything qualitative vanishes. We are left with empirical reality that we can manipulate ever more efficiently with technology.

Reality, as Kierkegaard notes, is comprised of necessity and possibility.[15] Necessity brings possibility to life. Possibility exists in imagination and desire, e.g., my future career; necessity is the means and will to make this possibility a reality. Freedom consists of both necessity and possibility. For the individual, freedom involves my supplying the necessity of will to turn a new possibility into actuality (reality). Without possibility we live an existence in which everything is determined and beyond my control, without necessity we live in a world of fantasy, of endless unfulfilled possibilities. Ellul has demonstrated that today every possibility is technological so that possibility has become necessity.[16] But the other side is equally important. When every skill has become technical, when all advice is expertise, when intelligence is "artificial," when all important decisions in my life are made for me by bureaucrats, then I have become an absent "ghost in the machine." I have vacated my own life of experience and practical knowledge and must live elsewhere. The media is not merely a choice but a necessity. Virtual reality is better than no reality. Necessity and possibility have become one.

I no longer have control over my life at the same time I have an overwhelming need to escape the hyper-rationalized society of rules and demands that we process ever more information ever more rapidly. Burdened by this enormous stress, we seek escape in our media culture, whose principal purposes are escape and compensation. In the social and mass media, I can become whatever

15. Kierkegaard, *Sickness Unto Death.*
16. Ellul, *Technological Bluff.*

and whoever I wish to be.[17] The media offers me endless possibilities: celebrity, superhero, demon, angel, monster, and so forth. Where once the visual image seemed to have a one-to-one relationship to empirical reality, it is now even more about possibility. There is no necessary relationship between the artificial (humanly constructed) visual image and reality.

Visual images hit us first at an emotional level.[18] Studies have indicated that the images that produce the strongest emotional response—violent images—are perceived to be most real.[19] The difference between reality and possibility is blurred. If visual images that bear no relationship to reality produce an emotional response, then they are emotionally real. The more we live in and through visual images, the more our emotions dominate our perception of reality. Omnipresent visual images in the media leave us vulnerable to advertising and propaganda and their universes of possibility, for which emotional arousal is their currency of manipulation. The more unfulfilled our lives, the more fear and anxiety gnaw at our sense of security, the more we turn to the media. Reality is in the media, but reality turns into possibility, as reality television demonstrates. Without transcendent truth as a check on reality, there is nothing to prevent reality from tilting in the direction of mere possibility.

Barfield's theory of symbolization and conceptualism stops with the triumph of positivism. Not long afterwards came structuralism, which denied the autonomy of the individual and the effectiveness of reason. Unconscious cultural structures obliterated the individual's freedom and reason. Postmodernism, which is the ideological reflection of a technological society without a common culture, puts to death our claim to interpret reality and establish a standard of truth. It rejects the ability of individual reason to interpret discourse validly. The inherent ambiguity of meaning in natural language makes a perfect interpretation impossible, but supplying the context of discourse can permit better

17. Martin, *Who Am I?*
18. Gombrich, "Visual Image."
19. Cited in Stivers, *Culture of Cynicism*, 154–57.

or worse interpretations. Postmodernism rejects even the latter. Postmodernism represents an attack upon language and the concept of truth. It rejects cultural authority in the name of cultural equality. At its extreme, postmodernism regards all art forms, all moralities, all meanings, all interpretations, as equal. Literature, art, and language, in their fragmentation and movement toward nihilism, give weight to the assertions of postmodernism. Recall van den Berg's discussion of multivalency. The animus of postmodernism is directed against the ideal of truth. When reason and discourse do not permit us to establish a standard of truth, then truth becomes political. All our concepts and facts become political. Witness the Trump administration's attack on environmental and medical science.

Reality has become ever more incomprehensible. The technological society is comprised of applied science (technology) that requires specialized knowledge. Even the specialist only fully understands her own specialty. Beyond it she is ignorant of the specialized knowledge that informs decision-making. Yet we need to know what is going on around us. Sound bites reduce knowledge to its lowest common denominator—an emotional response of for or against. And this response translates into a political response.

In *The Power Elite*, C. Wright Mills revealed that corporate, political, and military leaders do not openly conspire to increase their power at our expense but rather act out of common purpose: a tacit conspiracy of common interests in retaining and expanding their power.[20] They have no need of secret meetings when they are already in agreement about a common goal.

Power, however, has become abstract in a technological society: it resides in the technological system and the bureaucratic political state. Power is in the whole—the system. The rich and the powerful have greater access to this power and benefit from it much more than the rest of us, but the power itself does not reside in their person, office, or knowledge. Power is technical expertise apart from human experience. We do not understand power and we cannot tolerate living in an abstract society where there is no

20. Mills, *Power Elite*.

one to blame when things go wrong; consequently, we need an explanation we can understand. Conspiracy theory provides both—an explanation and someone to blame, the scapegoat.

Governments operate in as much secrecy as possible, if only for purposes of national security. Increasingly though it would appear that everything has become a matter of national security. When we do not know what government is up to, along comes a conspiracy theory to reveal its secrets. Specialized knowledge, abstract power, common interest, and secrecy leave us at the mercy of conspiracy theories. For decades before the coming of social media, novels, movies, and television programs have shown us imagined conspiracies of those in government, the military, the police, and in corporations. The social media spreads and extends conspiracy theories to every aspect of life.

In *The Political Illusion*, Ellul argued that only political facts are taken seriously, but now all facts have become political.[21] So if truth, reality, and facts are all political, where is there common ground for dialogue? The number of people who still hold on precariously to the idea of truth that is not political is diminishing. Without a shared reality based on truth, we inhabit mutually exclusive groups, each with its own version of truth and reality.

Edwin Lemert's study of those labeled paranoid schizophrenic illustrates our present situation.[22] Lemert examined the cases of patients who were diagnosed as paranoid schizophrenic and subsequently placed in mental institutions. Each of the patients had a story about friends and co-workers conspiring against him. Lemert discovered that, indeed, there had existed a conspiracy against the paranoid. Early on, the paranoid person had experienced turmoil in his life and became unfriendly and critical of those close to him, in many instances, co-workers, who, in turn, had meetings about what to do about the once friendly but now unfriendly co-worker. Unable to normalize his unruly behavior, they conspired to minimize contact with him. The more the paranoid person was excluded from group activities and communication,

21. Ellul, *Political Illusion*.
22. Lemert, "Dynamics of Exclusion."

the more confrontational he became, in part to force co-workers to communicate with him once again. When we inhabit mutually exclusive domains, communication ceases. Or should I say it becomes accusatory.

Applied to political conflict today, we can say that our opponents in competing political groups become scapegoats for the important problems society faces. They conspire to harm us and society at large. The main function of social media is to create online mobs, who spread rumors, make accusations, and promote conspiracy theories. Without a common morality and common understanding of truth, reality, and fact, we inhabit mutually exclusive universes where those who disagree with us are our enemies. Our common enemy, the scapegoat, is what unites us. Our enemies are members of a different race, ethnic group, gender, age group, and especially political party. As Peter Pomerantsev argues in *This is Not Propaganda*, conspiracy theory is now the central component of ideology.[23] What holds our group together is the belief that our common enemy, the scapegoat for our troubles, is conspiring against us. Conspiracy theory is the story of what the scapegoat has done and his plans for the future.

The popularity of media stars such as Jack Posobiec and Alex Jones indicates how widespread the belief in conspiracy theory is: it has moved into the mainstream of America. A recent survey indicated that approximately half of those surveyed believed in at least one of the five leading theories of the political Left or at least one of the five leading theories of the political Right.[24] There is a direct relationship between cultural fragmentation and the popularity of conspiracy theories.

The QAnon movement is attempting to create a master conspiracy theory that explains everything that troubles anyone. Growing in popularity, it has become an openly religious movement with a theory that, borrowing from certain fundamentalist groups, predicts an apocalyptic end of the world and subsequent

23. Pomerantsev, *This is Not Propaganda*.
24. Oliver and Wood, "Conspiracy Theories."

89

rebirth.[25] This movement cuts across ideological lines, indicating one frightening way America could be united again.

In *Propaganda*, Ellul distinguishes between agitation propaganda and integration propaganda.[26] The former is propaganda directed against one's enemies, whether in or out of government. Integration propaganda aims to unify a society around a certain ideological or mythological belief. The long-term success of integration propaganda is more difficult to achieve than the short-term success of agitation propaganda that arouses the crowd to hate the enemy. With no unity possible today without finding a universal and permanent scapegoat, the political party in power must rely on agitation propaganda that is relentless in mobilizing the true believers of the party against the enemy. Omnipresent conspiracy theory turns possibility into a schizophrenic reality.

## The New Left and the New Right

The New Political Left and the New Political Right are only the most religious of the political movements in America. The traditional Political Left and the traditional Political Right could occasionally get along; not so the New Political Left and New Political Right today. Both are fundamentalist religious movements that reject compromise.

The American political scene features a myriad of single-issue voters and their causes. Some issues, like abortion and gun rights, dominate media coverage. In each case, there are passionate opponents and proponents. For every governmental regulation there is an opponent and where there is no regulation an advocate for one. Single-issue voters often find a temporary abode in a larger political movement and sometimes in a political party. The single issue defines what proponents or opponents consider to be of supreme importance.

25. LaFrance, "Nothing Can Stop"; see also Barkun, *Culture of Conspiracy*.
26. Ellul, *Propaganda*.

The single issue is symbolic along the lines of the temperance movement of the late nineteenth and early twentieth centuries. Joseph Gusfield demonstrated that by the time the Volstead Act was passed in 1919, drinking was less problematic than it had been in previous decades. The temperance movement, he argued, was symbolic of small-town, Protestant, middle- and working-class America over against urban, Catholic, immigrant America. Anti-drinking was more about those who used it than about drink itself.[27]

There are now two symbolic movements, one on the Left and one on the Right, that are most contentious and religiously fundamentalist. They are moralistic and authoritarian in the desire to impose their agenda on the rest of society. Their rigidity brooks no compromise. They wish to define what America should be. But there are other groups in the political mix as well.

On the Right there is the traditional pro-business voting block. They are opposed to government regulating business but in favor of welfare in the form of tax cuts and incentives. On the Left, a voting block that advocates on behalf of working people, trade unions, and, at times, on behalf of the poor. These two blocks make up what has been the backbone of the two political parties for well over a century. From the 1980s Christian conservatives, who were opposed to abortion, homosexuality, and other forms of personal immorality, tended to join the Republican Party with its pro-business agenda. Progressive Christians, who supported social justice and equality, were inclined to support the Democratic Party.

The Techno-Libertarians are newer to the scene. They have some things in common with the Left and some things with the Right. They tend to vote for the Democratic Party, favoring greater equality for minority groups, women, and the poor. Concurrently however, they are opposed to the governmental regulation of the technology sector of the economy and unionization of their employees. They favor both equality and freedom, but at closer examination, freedom for themselves and an equality as homogenization that technology imposes on its users for everyone else.

27. Gusfield, *Symbolic Crusade.*

For them the Internet is the realization of the American Dream of freedom and equality for everyone.

This leaves us with the two most important political (religious) movements, passionately opposed to one another in the attempt to define America. One looks to the past, one to the future. One is nostalgic, one is utopian. But both are populated by fundamentalists, some of whom are rigid, moralistic, and authoritarian in intention. And both force their more moderate allies to accommodate them.

The New Left advocates for cultural and political equality. They want economic equality, of course, but more than that they want an equality of race, ethnicity, gender, sexual identity, and moral choice. They oppose all forms of discrimination and prejudice against minorities of every kind. They support "political correctness" but want much more than this: greater sensitivity to the other even when no overt prejudice has been expressed. They desire an end to all cultural distinctions that are based on inequality. Total equality is the value that unites the group, but their strident approach has alienated some on the Left who believe economic equality should be the main emphasis because, in their view, the other equalities are based on it. Moreover, the latter fear that the white poor and white working class will resent the heavy emphasis on minorities, especially minorities of sexual preference and identity.

Those on the New Right want to "make America great again," and are, for the most part, supporters of Donald Trump. Many are white men, who resent the attention given to minorities, and yearn for a time after World War II when there was an abundance of good-paying jobs and everyone accepted the cultural distinctions of the time. They perceive that their own worth is being diminished by the political correctness movement and that they are now losers—white men, vilified by their treatment of minorities, with no future.

The New Right appears to be a cultural revitalization movement, as Anthony Wallace has described it.[28] When material

28. Wallace, *Death and Rebirth.*

hardship and poverty are combined with demoralization and a diminished sense of worth revitalization movements emerge almost spontaneously. A leader of the movement, both religious and political, points the way to bring the group and its culture back to its former glory. Wallace discusses how the Seneca prophet Handsome Lake in the early nineteenth century, in the face of white settlers encroaching on their land and traditional way of life, developed a program of collective self-improvement that would allow a return to a time when their culture was vibrant and they had confidence in themselves.

Gun rights is the key symbolic issue for the New Right movement. It allows them to return to a time when there was little if any objection to gun ownership. Gun ownership confers dignity on those who refuse to be pushed around. Anti-government fervor is concentrated in the freedom to own and use guns. For them it is an absolute right, a freedom without responsibility to others. The gun is a symbol of their protection against government, which has entangled their lives in a large net of rules without benefit to them. Moreover, government has taken what little they had and given it to minorities. The New Right has drawn a line with gun rights, a line that an oppressive government must not cross. One of my relatives, a lifetime NRA member, said if the government came to take her guns, she would board up her windows and be prepared for a shoot-out. She was a modern-day Patrick Henry. What connects gun rights and resentment of minorities is the belief that the same government that has given their jobs to minorities wants to take away their right to own guns. This government wants to take away their freedom.

The New Right is against expertise and the experts who tell them what to do, whether not to pollute or use fossil fuels. Governmental regulations and the advice of expertise are perceived as external rules without immediate benefit to them. Enormous inequality in America leads to a diminished sense of community, anger at being looked down upon, and a resentment of authority.[29] The one thing left to the disenfranchised is to say no to a rule that

29. Wilkinson and Pickett, *Spirit Level*.

harms their lifestyle. Government, it appears to them, makes use of experts to further limit their few remaining freedoms.

One belief that all on the Right share is that government has too many regulations and threatens them with even more. It is easier to unite a group around what they are opposed to than what they support. The propaganda of the Right is directed against government in and of itself, not a particular government. The Right has made government into a scapegoat. A positive goal immediately presents problems of implementation. And the more ambitious the goal the greater obstacles there are to its realization. Hence, the Political Right advocating against big government has an advantage over the Political Left that promotes equality.

Over the years critics have termed the conflict between the New Left and the New Right "culture wars."[30] This is correct as far as it goes. But I think there is an even larger issue at work. One group, the supporters of "make America great again," want to return to the past. Like all rebellions, the New Right Movement looks backward to an idealized past.[31] The New Left looks to a utopian future that technological progress will create. In that sense it mimics revolution that is invariably about the future.

Louis Dumont captures the essence of the two movements in his contrast between the traditional ideology of hierarchy and holism and the modern ideology of equality and individualism.[32] Hierarchy and holism go together in the following way. There is no social order (holism) without cultural authority. Some statuses are higher than others, e.g., old is higher than young, male is higher than female (sometimes it is the reverse). Some have speculated that the original division of labor between the old and the young and between men and women in the milieu of nature pitted short-term survival, that is, the physical strength of men and the wisdom of age, against long-term survival, that is, the procreation of children and the stamina of youth.[33] The statuses that represent

---

30. Hunter, *Culture Wars*.

31. Ellul, *Autopsy of Revolution*.

32. Dumont, *From Mandeville to Marx*.

33. Ellul, *What I Believe*, 104–14.

short-term survival were given slightly higher status in that they were more representative of the whole, the community. This is why, Dumont maintains, the word *man* originally meant both man as a sexual identity and man as a designation of both sexes. The authority of the higher status was easily contested, however.

The statuses are held together by a morality that does not so much proscribe and prescribe the behavior of individuals toward other individuals, but of status groups in relation to complementary groups, e.g., young to old, female to male. The moral demands are reciprocal. The idea of complementarity suggests that it takes both young and old, female and male to make a community. What holds hierarchy together is holism. The sense of the whole, the community, takes precedence over and mitigates differences in status and power between complementary groups. When the system works well, differences of status are more pronounced than those of power. When the system begins to weaken in the milieu of society with the division of labor becoming more extensive and social hierarchy more rigid, then differences in status and power become greater. At this time the principle of holism starts to become subordinate to that of hierarchy. The inequality of hierarchy takes precedence over the equality of holism. Yet there is no holism without hierarchy: this is the fundamental idea.

The "make America great again" movement, the New Right, is a nostalgic revisiting of America in the 1950s when women and minorities knew their place in the social hierarchy and did not challenge it. It was a time when moral norms and proper sexual identity were widely accepted. In this idealized view of America, the New Right movement fails to recognize that differences in status and power had become so great that a sense of the whole community had begun to vanish. It refuses to recognize and remember genocide against Native Americans, brutal slavery and continuous institutionalized discrimination against Blacks, discrimination against immigrants, and turning women into indentured servants. White men in particular want their status and power back. They perceive that the pursuit of greater equality is at their expense.

Modern ideology (in the milieu of technology), Dumont explains, is based on the values of equality and individualism. Without holism and hierarchy, each status group is in competition with its former complement, young and old, female and male. Normative relations are now competitive and anomic (normless). The competition for power is endless, for no dominant group can claim legitimacy for its power. Even majority rule violates the value of holism. The majority in a democracy, Tocqueville points out, tends to be tyrannical. Government and public opinion, controlled by those temporarily in power, suppress minority views by threatening them with social isolation. Majority rule does not create holism but an enforced order.

Lawrence Friedman calls modern society the horizontal society because it is comprised of special interest groups (formerly status groups), which exist to further the rights of the individuals who identify with them.[34] These special interest groups compete for support and access to power. At bottom these groups are peopled by individuals who are psychologically autonomous. Moreover, the individual has an impersonal relationship to the group. The individuals within the group are often in competition to have the group express their desires. In a hierarchical society, individuality is kept under control by a sense of the whole and one's status within it. In modern societies individuality is autonomous only to be vulnerable to the collective force of public opinion. Holism and hierarchy give way to individualism and collectivism at the expense of community. The New Left movement exemplifies modern ideology. Racial, ethnic, age, sexual identity, and moral freedom groups work on behalf of their advocates.

Modern ideology as expressed in the New Left has to be understood in the context of a technological system and its impact on politics, just as the return to an idealized America of the New Right does. Power has become abstract and resides in the technological system and in the heavily technicized political state. The power of technology is the power of efficiency. And this means everything has to be measured for the sake of a technical logic. Even

34. Friedman, *Horizontal Society.*

human qualities, such as love and happiness, must be taken out of context, which gives them meaning, and rendered scalable. This is part of the homogenization of reality—the reduction of everything to empirical reality. Every technique, which objectifies both user and recipient, replaces meaning, experience, and judgment with a life that neatly fits into statistical categories.

The technological system demands the equality of measurement for purposes of efficiency and control: homogenized humans are required. We can differ in the amount of, let us say, happiness, but happiness must be homogeneous not qualitatively different for each individual. The only true conformity today is conformity to technology, as Ellul observes.[35] At the same time, however the technological system can permit virtually any aesthetical or ethical view, for these do not threaten the system. Witness the choices about what constitutes art or ethics, choice about sexual identity and sexual standards, choice about what a family is, choice about whether to use logic or not. This cultural chaos does not threaten the technological system over which culture can no longer exercise control. Cultural chaos is not control. The political movement for equality is in harmony with the equality that the technological system requires.

Political equality is not technological equality, however. The power of technology exacerbates political tensions and conflicts in the absence of cultural authority. Each special interest group is competing for power and access to greater resources. Short of totalitarian control the political state has limited ability to make equality a reality. Equality of opportunity is a chimera. For example, how do you give children an equal chance in life? To do so would require that all children have parents who employ an exact, technical method of parenting. But the methods of parenting in the real world exist within an infinitely complex emotional context. Clearly there is no one way of being a parent, even of a parent who maximizes the child's chances for success. Do we wish to bus children to different households, not just to different schools?

---

35. Ellul, *Technological System*.

Government has two major ways of promoting equality. First, it makes political correctness more or less mandatory. Second, it can emphasize statistical representation. For example, some suggest that women and men should receive the same pay and an equal rate of promotions for the same job as measured in the aggregate by outcome not opportunity. Because outcome is often an indicator of historical discrimination, equal aggregate outcome is a norm that overtakes equality of opportunity. The new norm negates individual differences: The individual becomes an equal member of a statistical category. Statistical categories are easier to control than individuals.

The "make America great again" movement, the New Right, resents the various forms of cultural and political equality. They oppose governmental regulations in support of equality. They do not realize that government is implementing the equality the technological system demands. The rebellion of the New Right, opposed to the revolution of the New Left, represents an attempt to restore a hierarchy of race, ethnicity, and gender and the accompanying morality that limits moral choice. The New Left is in the vanguard of technological progress. The New Right, while not opposed to technology itself, wants to negate the social consequences of technological progress. They do not realize that technological progress requires that society be in conformity with the logic of homogenization. The New Right and the New Left are religious movements that make stronger social demands than traditional religions can today. They indicate that nothing gets accomplished outside of politics.

## The Political Party as Church

The New Left is a loosely organized religious movement. It does not have a single religious leader, for it has as many spokespersons as it does special interest groups, each demanding equality. The New Left as a whole has a thinner layer of agreement than the New Right, because equality is more a symbol than a plan for action.

The advantage of the New Right is that it functions as a tightly organized religion with a church.

The Democratic Party is more like the Protestant church with its different denominations, the Republican Party, more like the Catholic Church with its unified policies. The Republican Party has become a church that has been taken over by the Trump sect. The parallels drawn between political and religious organizations as institutions and their rituals are not far-fetched if we keep in mind the functions they both perform.[36] The common functions: socialize members in a belief system; create a code of ethics or a platform; demand obedience to the authority of the church or party; establish rituals, such as holy days or holidays; and present believers with a happy future in this world or the next. The political church needs to align itself with the nation as a whole. Its cause is the nation's cause. Within the church are the clergy, the various leaders of the Republican party. The leaders include those in the legislative branch of government from the national to the local level, those who form the executive branch, and those functionaries whose task is the day-to-day operations of the party from fundraising to election campaigns. The clergy is not organized in a perfect hierarchy like that of the Catholic Church, but an irregular one in which certain state politicians, notably governors, can rise suddenly to greater prominence on the national scene. They are perceived as the future stars of the party.

The laity includes those who register as Republicans, especially those who vote in the primaries. Like most churches today the Republican Party welcomes the occasional churchgoer, those who perform the political ritual of voting only on occasion, or who are merely sympathetic with the party on a single issue, e.g., immigration.

The liturgy of the Republican church is contained in Trump's political rallies, which are truly religious revivals. There is a long-standing history of religious revivals in America. In the nineteenth century preachers would hold tent meetings, revivals that lasted several days or more. The goal was to stir the crowd to greater

36. Ellul, *New Demons*.

fervor and commitment. The preacher was only as good as his ability to arouse the crowd. If he could do this, he became a star and his fame preceded him as he moved from location to location. President Trump's rallies are almost identical. Like the prophet Handsome Lake,[37] prophet Trump preaches revitalization, "make America great again." Trump praises good—his views—and rails against evil—the views of his enemies. The number of his enemies is legion: the "deep state," Democrats, liberals, socialists, immigrants, minorities, losers, and so on. For Trump the prophet the conflict between Republicans and Democrats is a religious war. Trump has been able to figure out what others have not: politics is religion.

Consciously aware of his ability to manipulate a crowd, Trump fosters the cult of personality, the cult of the hero. How else can one make sense of the recent image of him standing in front of a vacated church with Bible in hand? Like authoritarian leaders before—Mussolini, Hitler, Stalin, and Mao, and current authoritarian leaders he admires, Putin and Kim—Trump portrays himself as a savior, who god-like, can lead believers to the promised land, a paradise in this world.[38] Like all authoritarian leaders he emphasizes what a threat his enemies pose. They conspire to ruin his plans to "make America great again." Trump is the master scapegoater, who perceives conspiracies everywhere.

But Trump can't do it alone; he needs an office or ministry of propaganda. The purpose of the Catholic Church's office of propaganda in the seventeenth century was the evangelization of non-Catholic countries. The purpose of Trump's ministry is internal: propaganda has to be continuously foisted on the American public. Fox News is his ministry of propaganda. Like Pravda (Putin is one of his heroes) it communicates what Trump wants it to say. His words are infallible. Trolls and disinformation consultants aid

---

37. Wallace, *Death and Rebirth*.

38. For some Christians the promised land in this world is a Christian one. Rick Perry has anointed Trump the "chosen one" to lead America back to its Christian foundation.

and abet Fox News and the Republican Party.[39] No rumor and no conspiracy theory is too outrageous.

The mainstream media as well are under his control. By giving him constant publicity, almost all of which is helpful (publicity in and of itself is beneficial), and by normalizing his words and actions in reporting them in a "neutral" way, the mainstream media make it appear that at most Trump is unusual or eccentric rather than being obviously sociopathic.

The Republican Party's platform is like many religious teachings abstract to the point of being vague. What matters most to the church as a religious institution is its moral norms about everyday actions and attitudes. Trump's "moral" message is that our enemies, everyone who opposes us in any way, conspire against us daily. We have to identify our enemies (scapegoats) and unite against them. Trump unifies less by telling his congregation what to believe, "make America great again," than by what they should oppose. President Trump is a connoisseur of conspiracy theories and shrewdly realizes that all conspiracy theories, both those on the Right and the Left, benefit him, just as he realizes that all media attention is helpful. If we live in a world of conspiracies, only an authoritarian leader can restore order.

The Republican Party has an advantage over the Democratic Party insofar as it is a church. The Republican Party advocates *freedom*—freedom of business, religious freedom, and freedom from governmental regulations. The Democratic Party makes *equality* its paramount value, whether economic equality or cultural equality or both. There is only one political faction that advocates both freedom and equality—the Techno-Libertarians. While demanding unrestricted freedom for those in the technology sector, they offer us the superficial freedom to collect and disseminate information on the Internet at the same time they impose a technological homogeneity on us. Is this faction our future?

---

39. Pomerantsev, *This is Not Propaganda.*

CONCLUSION

# The Semblance of Christianity

In *Protestant, Catholic, Jew*, Herberg understood that Protestant, Catholic and Jewish religions had become denominations within the American Way of Life, a secular religion, one part civic religion that featured a belief in American democracy and capitalism, and one part personal religion that fostered religion as peace of mind. His 1955 book was prescient. Ellul's two sacred axes, technology/sex, violence and the nation-state/revolution are finally what enables us to understand these two types of religion. They are not merely two choices within a myriad of religious choices. No, they are *the* religions. Christianity now makes its living within the boundaries of these dominant religions.

Today there are conservative, progressive, and moderate Christians. Conservative and progressive Christians are the most religious, that is, political of the denominations. Conservative and progressive Christians reflect the positions of the New Right and the New Left. In both instances, Christianity has been reduced to morality and morality to a few symbolic issues that are to be approached politically. Religion is always easier to stomach if it makes minimal requirements on one, that is, supporting a few symbolic issues. Progressive Christians lobby to have their agenda of cultural, political, and economic equality imposed on the nation, whereas conservative Christians push to have their anti-abortion, anti-homosexuality, pro-gun rights agenda become the law of the land. The point is not that Christians should not be involved in politics or that the church should never take a political stand but that politics has taken over from the institution of religion as the all-encompassing form of social control. Today the political process is all-consuming and the acquisition of power is an end in itself. When religion becomes a social institution, it is already a nascent political institution.

*pedantic*

Concomitantly, personal religion has transformed Christianity into a means to acquire a state of well-being, a mild ecstatic state of mental health or happiness. Christians are in the forefront of self-help books on piety and spirituality. Christianity is thereby reduced to a psychological technique, which is necessary to help us adjust to the demands of a technological society.

Jacques Ellul offers us an explanation of these two divergent religions co-existing in the present.[1] As a historian he argues that in a time of cultural chaos authoritarian religious and political movements arise to reestablish order. A technological society lacks a common morality and is culturally fragmented. Fundamentalist religious groups and authoritarian political leaders rise to meet the challenge. The New Right with its authoritarian leader represents an attempt to reestablish "law and order."

Concurrently, in a time of the near totalitarian control by the technological system and the political state, movements develop to allow people to escape the totalitarianism. Mystical self-transformation and the pursuit of ecstasy with speed and violent images are the avenues of escape that personal religion offers. What makes our situation unique is that we have a society that is chaotic on the cultural level and totalitarian at the technological level. Consequently we need both radically different types of religion.

In the final chapter of his book, Herberg abandoned his role as sociologist and spoke as a believer who understood both Judaism and Christianity. He argued that the American Way of Life was a form of idolatry. Our idols were America and the individual human. What about today? Karl Barth claimed that in the stupidity

---

1. Ellul, *What I Believe*, 125–27.

of sin we become practical atheists.[2] Politics as religion has institutionalized stupidity and turned us all into practical atheists. Our type of atheism is simultaneously a form of idolatry. We are still an idolatrous nation with a demagogue posing as a savior but in reality playing the part of Satan the accuser and the devil the divider. Paralyzed in our technological slumber, our lives filled with fantasy and escapism, we have to be awakened from this religious nightmare.

Some believed that if Trump was voted out of office, politics would return to normal, but Trump has been coming for a long time. With the universal and constant bombardment of propaganda, advertising, and public relations, truth and reality have gone into hiding. All facts have been politicized. We are vulnerable to every rumor, every bit of disinformation, every conspiracy theory. How can we decide what is true and what is false? But yet we must choose, for it is unbearable to live in a permanent state of confusion. Only conspiracy theories can organize the chaos of conflicting information on the Internet. We witness the rise of authoritarian political leaders and fundamentalist religious movements on the Right all over the world, fueled in part by anti-immigrant sentiment. What better scapegoat than the immigrant?

Democracy is dead. It was never more than partially realized before. Democracy is contradicted by technology, bureaucracy, and the media. How can we make informed decisions when only experts understand the technology and science behind them? How can we make informed decisions when bureaucracy operates in secrecy? How can we make informed decisions when social and mass media feed us a steady diet of dramatized, superficial, and misleading information? How can we make informed decisions when political religion's fundamental appeal is irrational? We are starving for the truth but instead are put on a strict diet of slogans and sound bites.

Democracy lives as a vague memory, but some moral and political control of technology is necessary. The overwhelming task is not to oppose technology but the technological *system*.

2. Barth, *Church Dogmatics*, Vol. IV, Part 2.

The technological system is robbing us of our freedom and our humanity. Politics must be desacralized and reduced to a useful institution for achieving justice but nothing more. It is not the solution to all moral problems. It must return to being one institution among many.

For society to be ready for a nonviolent revolution, Ellul argues, two conditions must be present.[3] First, society as it is, must be incapable of meeting its members' needs. Second, people must sense that life has become psychologically and spiritually intolerable. As the environmental crisis deepens, global inequality increases, and with more pandemics in the offing, we are rapidly approaching the first condition. The sense of meaninglessness and hopelessness, however, is swallowed by our culture of escapism. We have an app for every fear, every anxiety, every disappointment. We have chosen to live virtual lives. Somehow our unconscious hopelessness must rise to the surface.

Our task is unprecedented, for we are not just up against an oppressive society but an oppressive milieu. Personal and political religion are part of our oppression. When religion is a social institution, it becomes a necessary ally of politics in an authoritarian society. In its totalitarian purview the technological society *requires* the assistance of political and personal religion. This message will drive many to denial and escapism, but there will undoubtedly be some who still relish a fight if only their experiences are clarified so that they can clearly understand what they must oppose. We await such a minority, for our freedom depends on it.

Should Christians participate in a secular resistance movement against totalitarianism? Christians must respect the authority of the political state when it limits its power to relative matters of law and justice. But when it seeks and demands adoration, when it embodies sacred power, and when it becomes an idol, Christians must resist. Withdrawing support of political religion is the first step toward freedom. Although Christian freedom[4] is radically

3. Ellul, *Autopsy of Revolution.*

4. Christians talk about religious freedom today but only in a superficial way. They usually mean that government should not hinder the conventional

different from secular freedom, there are times, and this is one, when Christians and non-Christians have a common interest in achieving freedom from totalitarian control. Christians can help non-Christians understand that authoritarian and totalitarian control is inevitably religious. In this way we will have discerned the spirits that both obfuscate reality and enslave us.

---

practice of their religion. That Christian freedom entails a radical opposition to the technological and political organization of America is anathema to them. Freedom, instead, means security within the confines of American institutions.

# Bibliography

Aron, Raymond. *Progress and Disillusion*. New York: Praeger, 1968.

Bailey, Sarah Pulliam, Julie Zauzmer, and Josh Dawsey. "Trump Mocks the Faith of Others. His Own Religious Practices Remain Opaque." *The Washington Post*, February 14, 2020. https://www.washingtonpost.com/religion/2020/02/14/trump-mocks-faith-others-his-own-religious-practices-remain-opaque/.

Barfield, Owen. *Saving the Appearances*. New York: Harcourt, Brace Jovanovich, 1957.

Barkun, Michael. *A Culture of Conspiracy*. Berkeley, CA: University of California Press, 2003.

Barth, Karl. *Church Dogmatics*. Vol. I, Part 2. Translated by G. T. Thomson and Harold Knight. Peabody, MA: Hendrickson, 2010.

———. *Church Dogmatics*. Vol. II, Part 2. Translated by G.W. Bromiley, et al. Peabody, MA: Hendrickson, 2010.

———. *Church Dogmatics*. Vol. IV, Part 2. Translated by Geoffrey Bromiley. Peabody, MA: Hendrickson, 2010.

Bellah, Robert. "Civil Religion in America." *Daedalus* 96 (Winter 1967) 1–21.

Bonhoeffer, Dietrich. *The Cost of Discipleship*. Translated by R. H. Fuller. Rev. and unabridged ed. New York: Collier/Macmillan, 1963.

Borger, Joyce. "Using Technology to Support Worship Leaders." *The Banner*, August 2020. https://www.thebanner.org/our-shared-ministry/2020/09/using-technology-to-support-worship-leaders.

Bultmann, Rudolph. *The Gospel of John*. Translated by G. R. Beasley-Murray. Eugene, OR: Wipf and Stock, 2014.

Butler, Jon. *Awash in a Sea of Faith*. Cambridge: Harvard University Press, 1990.

Caillois, Roger. *Man and the Sacred*. Translated by Meyer Barash. New York: Free, 1959.

Canetti, Elias. *Crowds and Power*. Translated by Carol Stewart. New York: Seabury, 1978.

Clark, Brian, and Matt Kuzcinski. "Living Out Our Faith in a Technological World." *The Banner*, August 2020. https://www.thebanner.org/our-shared-ministry/2020/08/living-out-our-faith-in-a-technological-world.

Christian Broadcasting Network. *The 700 Club.* https://www.cbn.com/700club/
ShowInfo/about.

Christian Coalition of America. http://www.cc.org/our_agenda?__cf_chl_jschl
_tk__=c35dab1d324e6f3f8b895a9249d25da9032d3b42-1599066484
-0-AWk4jTAsuBRySYwgt3un5olxO56hKo15fNoKBT_VDxIWrztMuP
3UeKFiuMT8jJrRgVY4eOBc3wjOdbhYPxkmMtT4Ekvq9NevzBKCoI
Sf-lm2RdBf6q9QDPUI79Inr5GPcGrdPsAXAi95NGdwzAIGtY7S6sW5
-rnlX2XDuyPFH9riyJJzANs6zcDlqqOHEoztCUhZ2bADmwUoURCOj
mKnQe85OlmdP6oSXVovNFIBuqOoMziKu4CatjdXqvdmiCvDdOCFG
VACobGaOgei-VealsYNsMIpGk5UbW8YhkiM-Vno.

Clausewitz, Carl von. *On War.* Edited and translated by Michael Howard and
Peter Paret. Vol. 1. Princeton, NJ: Princeton University Press, 1989.

Congressional Prayer Caucus Foundation. "About." http://cpcfoundation.com/
about.

Crump, David. *I Pledge Allegiance: A Believer's Guide to Kingdom Citizenship in
Twenty-first-century America.* Grand Rapids: Eerdmans, 2018.

Dobson, James. "Past Broadcasts." *Dr. James Dobson's Family Talk.* https://www.dr
jamesdobson.org/broadcasts/past-broadcasts.

Dreyfus, Hubert L. *On the Internet.* London: Routledge, 2001.

Du Mez, Kristin Kobes. *Jesus and John Wayne: How White Evangelicals Corrupted a Faith and Fractured a Nation.* New York: Liveright, 2020.

Duby, Georges. *The Age of the Cathedrals.* Translated by Eleanor Levieux and
Barbara Thompson. Chicago: University of Chicago Press, 1984.

———. *The Three Orders.* Translated by Arthur Goldhammer. Chicago: University of Chicago Press, 1980.

Dumont, Louis. *From Mandeville to Marx.* Chicago: University of Chicago
Press, 1977.

Dworkin, Ronald. *Artificial Happiness.* New York: Carroll and Graf, 2006.

Eliade, Mircea. *Patterns in Comparative Religion.* Translated by Rosemary
Sheed. New York: New American Library, 1974.

———. *The Sacred and the Profane.* Translated by Willard Trask. New York:
Harper and Row, 1965.

Ellul, Jacques. *Apocalypse: The Book of Revelation.* Translated by George W. Sch-
reiner, New York: Seabury, 1977.

———. *Autopsy of Revolution.* Translated by Patricia Wolf. New York: Knopf,
1971.

———. *The Ethics of Freedom.* Translated by Geoffrey Bromiley. Grand Rapids:
Eerdmans, 1976.

———. *The Humiliation of the Word.* Translated by Joyce Hanks. Grand Rapids:
Eerdmans, 1985.

———. *If You Are the Son of God.* Translated by Anne-Marie Andreasson
Hogg. Eugene, OR: Cascade, 2014.

———. *Living Faith: Belief and Doubt in a Perilous World.* Translated by Peter
Heinegg. New York: Harper & Row, 1983.

——. *The New Demons.* Translated by C. Edward Hopkin. New York: Seabury, 1975.

——. *On Freedom, Love, and Power.* Expanded ed. Translated by Willem Vanderburg. Toronto: University of Toronto Press, 2015.

——. *Perspectives on Our Age.* Edited by Willem Vanderburg. Translated by Joachim Neugroschel. New York: Seabury, 1981.

——. *The Political Illusion.* Translated by Konrad Kellen. New York: Vintage, 1967.

——. *The Politics of God and the Politics of Man.* Translated and edited by Geoffrey W. Bromiley. Grand Rapids: William B. Eerdmans, 1972.

——. *Propaganda.* Translated by Konrad Kellen. New York: Knopf, 1969.

——. *The Subversion of Christianity.* Translated by Geoffrey Bromiley. Grand Rapids: Eerdmans, 1986.

——. "Symbolic Function, Technology and Society." *Journal of Social and Biological Structures* 1 (1978) 207–18.

——. *The Technological Bluff.* Translated by Geoffrey Bromiley. Grand Rapids: Eerdmans, 1990.

——. *The Technological Society.* Translated by John Wilkinson. New York: Knopf, 1964.

——. *The Technological System.* Translated by Joachim Neugroschel. New York: Continuum, 1980.

——. *The Theological Foundation of Law.* Translated by Marguerite Wieser. New York: Seabury, 1969.

——. *To Will and to Do.* Translated by C. Edward Hopkin. Philadelphia: Pilgrim, 1969.

——. *What I Believe.* Translated by Geoffrey Bromiley. Grand Rapids: Eerdmans, 1989.

Fitzgerald, Frances. "Come One, Come All." *The New Yorker,* December 3, 2007, 46–56.

Franken, Al. *Lies and the Lying Liars Who Tell Them: A Fair and Balanced Look at the Right.* New York: Dutton, 2003.

Friedman, Lawrence. *The Horizontal Society.* New Haven, CT: Yale University Press, 1999.

Gaustad, Edward S. *Church and State in America.* 2d ed. Oxford: Oxford University Press, 1999/2003.

Geertz, Clifford. "Religion as a Cultural System." In *The Interpretation of Cultures,* 87–125. New York: Basic, 1973.

George, Susan E. *Religion and Technology in the 21st Century: Faith in the E-world.* Hershey, PA: Information Science, 2006. https://epdf.pub/religion-and-technology-in-the-21st-century-faith-in-the-e-world.html.

Girard, René. *The Scapegoat.* Translated by Yvonne Freccero. Baltimore: Johns Hopkins University Press, 1986.

Gleick, James. *Chaos: The Making of a New Science.* New York: Penguin, 1987.

Gombrich, E. H. "The Visual Image." *Scientific American* 227 (September 1972) 82–96.

Grudem, Wayne. *Politics According to the Bible: A Comprehensive Resource for Understanding Modern Political Issues in Light of Scripture.* Grand Rapids: Zondervan, 2010.

———. "Why Voting for Donald Trump Is a Morally Good Choice." *Townhall,* July 28, 2016. https://townhall.com/columnists/waynegrudem/2016/07/28/why-voting-for-donald-trump-is-a-morally-good-choice-n2199564.

Gusfield, Joseph. *Symbolic Crusade.* Urbana, IL: University of Illinois Press, 1963.

Haggard, Ted. "Presidential Message, National Association of Evangelicals." https://web.archive.org/web/20060307100634/http://nae.net/.

Herberg, Will. *Protestant, Catholic, Jew.* Garden City, NY: Doubleday, 1955.

http://open.lifechurch.tv.

https://open.life.church/.

http://sermonsnet.com.

http://www.preachersgoldmine.com. .

http://www.preachingtoday.com.

http://www.preachingtodaysermons.com.

http://www.searchgodsword.org.

http://www.sermoncentral.com.

https://www.logos.com/why-logos.

Hunter, James Davison. *Culture Wars.* New York: Basic, 1991.

Hutson, James H. *Church and State in America: The First Two Centuries.* Cambridge: Cambridge University Press, 2008.

Isaacs, Harold. *Idols of the Tribe.* New York: Harper and Row, 1975.

Jouvenel, Bertrand de. *On Power.* Translated by J. F. Huntington. Boston: Beacon, 1962.

Kelsen, Hans. *Society and Nature.* New York: Arno, 1978.

Kierkegaard, Søren. *The Concept of Anxiety.* Translated by Reidar Thomte. Princeton, NJ: Princeton University Press, 1980.

———. *For Self-Examination Judge for Yourself!* Translated by Howard Hong and Edna Hong. Princeton, NJ: Princeton University Press, 1990.

———. *The Point of View for My Work as an Author.* Translated by Walter Lowrie. New York: Harper and Row, 1962.

———. *The Sickness Unto Death.* Translated by Alastaic Hannay. New York: Penguin, 1989.

———. *Works of Love.* Translated by Howard and Edna Hong. New York: Harper Torchbooks, 1964.

Kundera, Milan. *Slowness.* New York: Harper Collins, 1996.

LaFrance, Adrienne. "Nothing Can Stop What is Coming." *The Atlantic* 325 (June 2020) 27–38.

Leibovitz, Liel. *God in the Machine.* West Conshohocken, PA: Templeton, 2013.

Lemert, Edwin. "Paranoia and the Dynamics of Exclusion." *Sociometry* 25 (March 1962) 2–20.

Lewontin, Richard. *Biology as Ideology.* New York: Harper Collins, 1991.

Luckmann, Thomas. *The Invisible Religion.* New York: Macmillan, 1967.

Marsh, Charles. "Wayward Christian Soldiers." *New York Times*, Op-Ed, January 20, 2005. https://www.nytimes.com/2006/01/20/opinion/wayward-christian-soldiers.html.

Martin, Jay. *Who Am I this Time?* New York: Norton, 1988.

Martínez, Jessica, and Gregory A. Smith. "How the Faithful Voted: A Preliminary 2016 Analysis." https://www.pewresearch.org/fact-tank/2016/11/09/how-the-faithful-voted-a-preliminary-2016-analysis/.

Marty, Martin. *A Nation of Behavers*. Chicago: University of Chicago Press, 1976.

Marty, Martin, and R. Scott Appleby. *The Glory and the Power*. Boston: Beacon, 1992.

Marvin, Rob. "Tech Addiction By the Numbers: How Much Time We Spend Online." *PC Magazine*, June 11, 2018. https://www.pcmag.com/news/tech-addiction-by-the-numbers-how-much-time-we-spend-online.

McLuhan, Marshall. *Understanding Media: The Extensions of Man*. New York: McGraw-Hill, 1964.

McNeil, Joanne. "Search and Destroy." *Harper's Magazine*, February 2020, 11–14.

Meyer, Donald. *The Positive Thinkers*. New York: Pantheon, 1965.

Mills, C. Wright. *The Power Elite*. New York: Oxford University Press, 1956.

Moore, Beth. Twitter. https://twitter.com/bethmoorelpm/status/939134068947550208?lang=en.

Morozov, Evgeny. *To Save Everything, Click Here*. New York: Public Affairs, 2013.

Nietzsche, Friedrich. *Thus Spoke Zarathustra*. Translated by Stephen Metcalf. Hollywood, FL: Simon and Brown, 2011.

———. *Vom Nutzen und Nachteil der Historie für das Leben (On the Use and Disadvantage of History for Life)*. In *Unzeitgemüße Betrachtungen (Untimely Observations)*, *Nietzsches Werke*, vol. 1. Edited by Elisabeth Förster-Nietzsche. Leipzig: Alfred Kröner, 1923.

Oliver, Eric, and Thomas Wood. "Conspiracy Theories and the Paranoid Style(s) of Mass Opinion." *American Journal of Political Science* 58 (October 2014) 952–66.

Pew Forum. "Faith on the Hill: The religious composition of the 116th Congress." January 3, 2019. https://www.pewforum.org/2019/01/03/faith-on-the-hill-116/.

———. "Religious Landscape Study." https://www.pewforum.org/religious-landscape-study/.

Pomerantsev, Peter. *This is Not Propaganda*. London: Faber and Faber, 2019.

Postman, Neil. *Amusing Ourselves to Death: Public Discourse in the Age of Show Business*. New York: Penguin, 1986.

Ricoeur, Paul. *Lectures on Ideology and Utopia*. Edited by George Taylor. New York: Columbia University Press, 1986.

Sahlins, Marshall. *Islands of History*. Chicago: University of Chicago Press, 1985.

Schüll, Natasha. *Addiction by Design*. Princeton, NJ: Princeton University Press, 2012.

Sharlet, Jeff. "Soldiers of Christ: Inside America's Most Powerful Megachurch." *Harper's Magazine*, May 2005. https://harpers.org/archive/2005/05/inside-americas-most-powerful-megachurch/.

Shellnut, Kate. "Make Worship Patriotic Again? The Top 10 Songs for Fourth of July Services." *Christianity Today*, June 29, 2018. https://www.christianitytoday.com/ct/2018/june-web-only/make-worship-patriotic-again-top-10-songs-fourth-of-july.html.

Siegel, Rachel. "Tweens, teens and screens: The average time kids spend watching online videos has doubled in 4 years." *Washington Post*, October 29, 2019. https://www.washingtonpost.com/technology/2019/10/29/survey-average-time-young-people-spend-watching-videos-mostly-youtube-has-doubled-since/.

Simondon, Gilbert. *On the Mode of Existence of Technical Objects*. Translated by Cecile Malaspina and John Rogove. Minneapolis: University of Minnesota Press, 2017.

Snaith, Norman. *The Distinctive Ideas of the Old Testament*. New York: Schocken, 1964.

"Stand for the Flag Kneel for the Cross T-Shirt." https://www.amazon.com/Stand-Flag-Kneel-Cross-Shirt/dp/B07NPLC4P4?customId=B0752XJYNL&th=1.

Stassen, Glen, and Lewis Smedes. "Confessing Christ in a World of Violence." 2004. https://odysseyblog.wordpress.com/2004/10/14/confessing-christ-in-a-world-of-violence/.

Steiner, George. *Real Presences*. Chicago: University of Chicago Press, 1989.

Stivers, Richard. *The Culture of Cynicism*. Cambridge: Blackwell, 1994.

———. "The Festival in Light of the Theory of the Three Milieus: a Critique of Girard's Theory of Ritual Scapegoating." *Journal of the American Academy of Religion* 61 (1993) 505–38.

———. *Shades of Loneliness*. Lanham: Rowman and Littlefield, 2004.

———. *Technology as Magic*. New York: Continuum, 1999.

*Time.* "The 25 Most Influential Evangelicals." Time Magazine. http://content.time.com/time/specials/packages/article/0,28804,1993235_1993243_1993280,00.html.

Tocqueville, Alexis de. *On Democracy in America*. 2 vols. Edited by Henry Reeve. New York: Vintage, 1945.

Tufte, Edward R. *The Cognitive Style of PowerPoint*. Cheshire, CT: Graphics, 2003.

Turkle, Sherry. *Alone Together*. New York: Basic, 2011.

Turner, Victor. *The Ritual Process*. Ithaca, NY: Cornell University Press, 1977.

Tuveson, Ernest. *Redeemer Nation*. Chicago: University of Chicago Press, 1968.

Vahanian, Gabriel. *The Death of God*. New York: Broziller, 1961.

Van den Berg, J. H. *The Changing Nature of Man*. Translated by H. F. Croes. New York: Norton, 1961.

van der Laan, J. M. *Narratives of Technology*. New York: Palgrave Macmillan, 2016.

Vonnegut, Kurt. *Hocus Pocus*. New York: G.P. Putnam's Sons, 1990.

Wallis, Jim. *God's Politics: How the Right Gets It Wrong and the Left Doesn't Get It*. New York: Harper Collins, 2005.

Wach, Joachim. *Sociology of Religion*. Chicago: University of Chicago Press, 1944.

Wallace, Anthony. *The Death and Rebirth of the Seneca*. New York: Vintage, 1969.

Watson, Colin P., Sr. "Technology: A Reality and a Gift." *The Banner* (August 2020). https://www.thebanner.org/our-shared-ministry/2020/08/technology-a-reality-and-a-gift. Retrieved 9/25/2020.

Whitehead, Andrew, and Samuel Perry. *Taking America Back for God*. New York: Oxford University Press, 2020.

Wilkinson, Richard, and Kate Pickett. *The Spirit Level*. New York: Penguin, 2010.

Wills, Garry. *What Jesus Meant*. New York: Penguin, 2006.

Woolley, Benjamin. *Virtual Worlds: A Journey in Hype and Hyperreality*. New York: Penguin, 1993.

Made in the USA
Monee, IL
21 November 2021

82680951R00083